Hearts of the Bible

The Good, the Bad, the Ugly

Volume one

By Dr. Michael R. Householder

Fishnet Publishers

100

Hearts from the Bible!

The Good, the Bad, the Ugly Ones

Volume One

Devotional Journal

Dr. Michael R. Householder

Devotions for the Heart

Volume One

Written by Dr. Michael R. Householder

Copyrighted 2014 by Fishnet publishers

and Dr. Michael R. Householder

Thanks to my wife Jacque for her help in devotional editing; and Lovella Richardson for editing.

Scripture quotations, unless otherwise indicated, are taken from the Holy Bible, New American Standard version.

Printed in United States of America

Fishnet Publishers

PO Box 20606

Knoxville TN, 37940

ISBN: 9781530633579

Dedication

I dedicated this series of books in loving memory of my Granddad,

John E. Settlemyer.

Of all the people I have ever known, my Granddad John had the heart of Jesus.

Contents _____

Preface

What is at the heart of the Bible? What is the heart of the gospel? What is the heart of what God wants from each of us? The answer to all is that God wants our hearts. I was reading the Word one day and kept reading about the hearts in the Bible. I then begin looking up how many hearts are mentioned. I searched and have found 270 different hearts in the Bible. Each one looks at different aspects of our life in God. But the Bible pulls no punches when doing so. It looks at the good, bad, and ugly heart. But many of us who claim to be a believer do not want to face the bad and ugly. Most people want to hear about the good heart but not the bad one. Since we have both natures, we have both kinds of heart. God tells us which heart is after His heart, and which is against, and in most cases how to have that kind of heart. The Bible is clear about bad and ugly hearts and the consequences of following hearts like that. Be not fooled; God does not want us to make a verbal commitment to Him without committing our heart. The great news is that if we are honest and truthful with ourselves, then we will approach Him with a natural bad heart in hope of having it turned into a good heart. As you read and study this book, my hope is that you take the good with the bad and know the difference. Also, that you be honest with your heart as it is, so that it can become what it should be with the power of his Spirit.

How can you get the most out of this book!

What do I hope you get out of this devotional book? In one word: **HONESTY.** The main thing is to wrestle with the text and questions, and be honest with yourself and God, or you will fail to benefit and grow from the experience.

Procedures: First, begin by praying, "Lord open my heart today as I look into your word." Second, read the passage given. Also, look at the verse in context to get a bigger picture. Third, just read through the devotional passage. Fourth, take each question in the body of the text and think about it, answering it honestly. Fifth, truly pray the prayer at the bottom of the page as well pray your prayer as you feel led. Sixth, answer the reflection questions on the next page, and then write down any thoughts you may have or answers to the other questions in the body of the text. Reflect on how the devotionals touched your heart or mind.

Small Groups Study: This book is also a great tool for small group discussions. After you read the passage and commentary go over each question, to explore and apply the heart to each person's life.

Sermon series: This is a great resource for a sermon series. As you study each heart, you will touch most subjects in the Bible. Have each person study the hearts for the week and use these devotions as a sermon starter.

From my heart to yours: be open, honest, and loving. Dr. Mike

This is a song I wrote while I was a missionary in Russia, hope you enjoy.

For the children with His heart!

1. Eyes have never seen, nor ears have ever heard

the wonders that are made

2. Look into his eyes and see His universe

See how it began and how He loved it so.

For the children with a heart,

children with His heart

CHORUS

The one who knows Him and loves Him. 2x

All He has is theirs

Today, tomorrow and forevermore

The one who knows Him and loves Him

3. Look into His eyes and see it through His soul

With love, He added color

in a rainbow in His sky

For the children with His heart

4. Hear the sounds of greatness, thunder claps its hands

But the wonders of their laughter is sweeter than before.
From the children with His heart

Children with His heart

Personal Reflections: What things do you see as a child of God?

_____

_____

_____

_____

_____

_____

_____

_____

_____

_____

_____

_____

_____

_____

_____

_____

_____

_____

_____

_____

_____

Introduction

Emotions and feelings cloud the modern day view of the heart "warm fuzzies" some might say). This concept is far different from the Hebrew's heart found in the Bible. I think the Biblical heart is more encompassing than just emotions or feelings. As you go through this devotional, you will discover the facets of the heart of man (generic term). The Biblical heart encompasses the total man, encompassing the center of man's existence. It may be more accurate to center the heart in one's mind. Because the Biblical heart, as you will see in this study, includes the area of thoughts, motivation, action, choice, courage, and will. It is the place for one's belief and understanding to radiate from in each of our lives. But you also cannot say it is just the mind. It is more, it is the control center of emotions, feelings, and it is the center of who we are as a person. It is what makes us different from all other living creatures. It is the thumbprint of God. It is where His image is evident in man. In Psalm 7:9 the English translates it "heart and mind," but the true translation is "kidney." The Hebrew was trying to get the center of man's innermost being. The kidney is used since it is in the middle of the body, although it is not as endearing or romantic as the heart. Even though it is the image of who God is, it is in each of our hands to determine how it is formed. What is done or chosen is each person's decision. Each person holds his or her destiny, whether to control yourself, give it to Satan or give it back to God. The result of self and Satan are the same. As you study, these passages let yourself be honest where you stand. For God is not fooled; He has already searched your heart and knows the intent and truth, or the lies that lie within your heart. This devotional includes both positive and negative aspects of the heart. As the Bible pulls no punches neither does this book. The hope is that as you read you will honestly look at your life with the hope of changing the negative into the positive.

Prayer: Lord, teach us what you know and the courage to be honest and change what you reveal, and the wisdom to know the difference between our world and His heart. In Jesus name, Amen.

Personal Reflections: What things do you have a problem being honest within your heart? What things have you overcome in your heart that is positive?

_____

_____

_____

_____

_____

_____

_____

_____

_____

_____

_____

_____

_____

_____

_____

_____

_____

_____

_____

_____

_____

Integrity of the Heart (Genesis 20:1-6)

6. Then God said to him in the dream, "Yes, I know that in the integrity of your heart you have done this, and I also kept you from sinning against Me; therefore I did not let you touch her.

Abimelech was a sincere and honest man. He was a man who was put in a difficult situation unknown to himself. To his knowledge, he was acting with a true and pure heart toward Abraham's wife/sister. The same was the case of Saul (Apostle Paul) when persecuting the Christians. Both men acted out of integrity of heart, and when shown the truth they both acted accordingly when God revealed the truth to them. God will give each person a way out as He did to these two Biblical examples. Once a person knows the impending danger and ignorance, it is up to them to act accordingly. Each person should ask: Is there anything in my life that I need revealed? Do I live and make decisions based on a heart of integrity, sincerity and truth? What things or attitudes should I change to be able to walk more uprightly? Show me what actions or events this past week where I either did or did not walk in integrity. One's true heart is not as evident when others can see you, but rather what you do and think when no one is around. Don't be fooled the first will soon be found out too, if the second is not true. We see in this passage that God knows and sees all that is in our hearts. We cannot hide from Him our motives, our thoughts, and our intentions. Everything is in His sight. Therefore, how should that cause us to live each day? Should it with lies and deceit, or with true integrity and honesty in our hearts? If God can see all, then why not be honest with self and others, and strive to do the right thing in our hearts.

Prayer: **Help me** to walk in integrity of heart every day in every way. **Show me** when I do or don't walk as I should. **Forgive me** for the times that I didn't resist the temptation. **Restore me** to a new heart. **Strengthen me** in spirit, so I will not fall into temptation. **Keep me** from sinning as you did with Abimelech.

Personal Reflections: What things do you struggle with in your thoughts that conflict with what you think is right? List some things that are right in your heart?

_____

_____

_____

_____

_____

_____

_____

_____

_____

_____

_____

_____

_____

_____

_____

_____

_____

_____

_____

Searching Heart (Deuteronomy 4:29)

" ... But from there you will seek the Lord your God, and you will find Him if you search for Him with all your heart and all your soul."

In this verse, we see the prediction of what was to be fulfilled in Jeremiah 29:11-13. The children of the promise got lost along the way when they sought after and followed other Gods, both in the wilderness, and years later in Israel. They stopped searching and began wandering. When you fail to search, then you either stay where you are or digress and wander after the first thing that comes along. It takes determination to search. It is not always easy and is most often time-consuming, but always worthy of our time and effort. For what we will find at the end of our search is wonders beyond our imagination; it is God. God wants to be found by those who search for him with all of their heart and soul. Each of us who wish to follow God must forsake other gods in our life, our time and agenda so that we can take control and search for the source of life. When we do, He promises to come to us, hear us, heal and bless us. Remember, "He is a rewarder of those who seek Him." **We need to ask:** Lord, reveal to me the other gods in my life. Lord, how can I seek with my whole heart and soul? What things do I do, or not do that hinder my search for you? God is not lost that you have to search for Him, but rather you need to search for Him because you are either lost or in need a deeper relationship. The Holy Spirit searches our thoughts and hearts to see who we are, and we should search for God to know who He is. How do we do this? We must read His Holy Word. In the Word, we see the mind and heart of God. We find Him because we make the effort to know God. Most do not make the effort because they think they are saved, and all else is optional. This is sad because we can never have enough of who God in Christ is. Our searching for God is not only about being saved it is about being in a relationship with God with all our heart.

Prayer: Help me to search for you with all my heart and soul. Help me to be honest in my walk and with myself. Lord, I repent of not searching for you, as I should. When I go astray, help me to come back to the true and narrow way. I praise you for helping me to search and find you.

Personal Reflections: What ways do you search God each day? Think of more ways to search for Him?

_____

_____

_____

_____

_____

_____

_____

_____

_____

_____

_____

_____

_____

_____

_____

_____

_____

_____

_____

_____

_____

Loving Heart (Deuteronomy 6:4-16)

5. "And you shall love the Lord your God with <u>all</u> your heart and with all your soul and with all your might."

When one usually thinks about contrasting the Old and New Testaments, one would describe OT as law and NT love. We find that this is not true. At the center of the Old Testament is God's love. It is the motivation of His people; it is also His hope for His people. From the beginning, God was all about love, even in his giving of the law and in His teachings. He never meant His people to obey, learn or teach the laws without love. We see this again in the phrases "all your heart and soul" and, in addition "all our might." Sometimes it takes all our strength or might to love someone. This of course applies when the person is not too loveable in our eyes. Due to our weakness of the flesh it takes all our might not to be unloving, even in relations to God. It should be when we think of God's love, commands, and laws we can love Him because we know that they are there for our benefit. He wants us to cling to Him to listen and follow His commands and teachings, not that of other gods. Deuteronomy 13:13 tells us that God is testing our love to see if it is genuine. Love is an action when we love we show God by following and being obedient to his teachings and commands. We see the importance of the words of Jesus when he says, "if you love me you will obey my teachings and commandments." God is not an agnostic, uninvolved God, but a God of Love and compassion and His desire is that His children, His creation love Him in turn. A loving God will not turn away a loving sinner. If we do not love Him, then our faith is an empty longing for salvation. Without a relationship with the Savior, the benefit of salvation is a moot point. Love for God should be the requirement for Him saving us. All means all. Short of this we fail to follow Jesus as the disciple we are called to do. God loves us so should we in return.

Prayer: Lord, help me see your love in all its facets. Help me not to see your commands as burdensome but loving. Forgive me when I don't love and cling only to you. Show me when I fail to love and how to correct it. Thanks for your love and understanding. Amen.

Personal Reflections: Make a list of ways you can love God each day. Pick one each day this week and show Him how you can love Him.

_____

_____

_____

_____

_____

_____

_____

_____

_____

_____

_____

_____

_____

_____

_____

_____

_____

_____

_____

_____

Proud Heart Deuteronomy 8:13-18

14 Then your heart became proud, and you forgot the Lord your God who brought you out from the land of Egypt, out of the house of slavery.

To look at this carefully, you might evaluate this problem as blindness or stupidity. Blind in that you convince yourself that what you've done was at the work of your hands. This is just plain stupidity because anyone in their right mind would not give credit to others when honor is due. We humans do tend to convince ourselves or lie to ourselves about the truth. Oh, how quickly do we forget how easy it is to call upon the Lord in times of need, and in times of plenty. I have often thought how the children of Israel could see all the miracles, and stand in the presence of God, and still claim arrogantly that they were the result of their efforts? I must beware that I too not fall into the trap when I am in prosperity. Or have run upon good fortune, to forget from where all blessings come, and the power or means of doing it. I must not forget that if I live, I live to the Lord, and if I die, I die to the Lord. In death or life, I am the Lord's. Uzziah became skilled and fruitful by the power of God, but when he became strong and famous he became proud and corrupted. What things/events in your life went great, and then you let pride take over and you forgot the person who truly made it possible? It may be a friend, a parent, and of course God. How do you think others feel when your pride overtakes the truth and their contribution? Just think about it. Lord, please reveal to me any pride that needs eliminating. Help me to see from whence comes my strength and never forget my origins, and that my worth comes through you. When you become prideful, you become forgetful that you're not God, and that you're not in control. When this happens, you forget all that God has done for you and through you, and you become the God of your life.

Prayer: Thank you, Lord, for everything that I am and any gift and talent I possess. Help me not to forget the good you do through me in everything, in every day. Help me not have any selfish pride about the things I accomplish. Praises to you O Lord from where comes my strength and power.

Personal Reflections: When have you not given credit to God? Remember all is on loan from God.

_____

_____

_____

_____

_____

_____

_____

_____

_____

_____

_____

_____

_____

_____

_____

_____

_____

_____

_____

_____

_____

_____

Serving Heart (Deuteronomy 10:12)

"And now Israel, what does the Lord your God require of you, but to fear the Lord your God, to walk in all His ways and love Him and to serve the Lord your God with all your heart and with all your soul.
Again, in this passage we see the Lord instructing His children in the way they should live. This time it is important to note the strong phrase "What does the Lord your God require of you," This is strong and forthright, almost demanding. Does God want a reluctant servant or a complaining servant or even a half-hearted servant that is forced to serve? No, from the beginning God wants His people to serve Him out of love. He wants them, though, to recognize that He is a mighty and awesome God that deserves their service. But most of all, He wants servants that are motivated from the heart. What is a half-hearted servant? How does the Father look upon the servant like this? A half-hearted servant is one that is lukewarm about his service. And we know God's opinion of the lukewarm Christian. What would it be like to serve God with joy without complaining? To serve with enthusiasm and not apathy, to serve with hope without wavering. To serve in partnership, and not isolation, to serve without looking to be served. Lord, search my heart that I may serve with my whole heart and soul. Lord, do I have to like the task to be able to serve with my whole heart? No, we do not because we must remember who we are serving. When we remember it is Jesus we serve and not the task, then we will have the fortitude to continue. Also, we must not serve to be recognized. Jesus tells us in Matthew 6 that if we do, then our reward is in the task and not for eternity. Loving to serve is God's hope for every disciple that follows Him. Serving is not always an easy thing to do since we live in the fleshly world, but if we keep in mind that He came to serve us first then we can do no less for Him.
Prayer: Lord always keeps me away from complaining while I serve. Forgive me when I don't serve with gladness and my all. Thank you for the joy You give in serving You. Thank you for even giving me the opportunity to serve, for it is such a privilege and honor. Lord help me to cope with those who make it difficult to serve as well as my preoccupation with my rights.

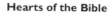

Personal Reflections: When was the last time you complained about serving? When was the last time you served with gladness of heart?

_____

_____

_____

_____

_____

_____

_____

_____

_____

_____

_____

_____

_____

_____

_____

_____

_____

_____

_____

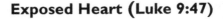

Exposed Heart (Luke 9:47)

"But Jesus knowing what they were thinking in their heart took the child and stood him by His side."

Some people claim to have the ability to read minds. Most people feel uncomfortable with the idea of having someone else read their mind or see deeply into their heart. They do so because they are afraid of what the other person might find out at any given moment. How would you feel if you knew your friend could read your mind at will? Would you find yourself avoiding that person for fear of what you might be thinking? Jesus was such a friend. In several cases, Jesus was noted for knowing what other people were thinking in their hearts. If you knew someone was listening, would you try to control your thoughts? Most play mind or heart games and are not honest with self and others. They convince themselves they are not thinking certain things, or they rationalize their thoughts. Some even try to suppress thoughts. I am one of those, and I think you are too. Jesus knows our hearts even when we try to hide it from others and even from ourselves. Be honest with yourself and do not try to deceive your heart/mind, for Christ knows it already. What things are you hiding in your heart? What things do you rationalize about that may stand in the way of your growth or mental health? Jesus wants you to be honest with yourself and Him because your salvation may be at stake. Jesus is concerned about our true heart. If our heart is not right, then we will not be right with God. If someone could see in your heart what would you do? Would you try to change and become what you should be? The opposite question is, if they could not see, would you still do what is right in the eyes of God? Transparency is the true test of your character and the righteousness' of your heart. God cares about this the most. Why do we play the mind games when we know He knows all?

Prayer: Lord, you can see inside me, so search me and help me to be honest with you and myself. I want to serve you sincerely. Help me to discern others' hearts as well so that I can help them in their growth. In your holy name, Amen.

Personal Reflections: What things do you try to hide from God? Why? Confess something that you hide.

_____

_____

_____

_____

_____

_____

_____

_____

_____

_____

_____

_____

_____

_____

_____

_____

_____

_____

_____

Wholehearted (Acts 8:37)

And Phillip said, "If you believe with your <u>whole heart</u> you may." And he answered and said, "I believe that Jesus Christ is the Son of God."

When I was growing up, I was taught "if it is worth doing it is worth doing right." Also, if you cannot do something with all your heart, it will not be all that it can be. The New Testament gives a prime example of not giving it your all. Jesus describes it as being lukewarm. In Revelation 3 we see the church of Laodicea about to be condemned for being lukewarm. They did not give or worship the Lord with a whole heart. God wants us to decide or commit to go all the way, or not at all. He wants us to go the whole nine yards. As a former football player, I would have said go the whole ten yards, but you get the idea. Philip told the eunuch that he would baptize him if he believed with his whole heart. God does not want half-hearted servant, but I am afraid that many pew sitters are just going through the motions of religious tradition, void of total surrender of their whole heart or lives. Philip did not want just a decision, but a total commitment to Jesus as Lord. It seems that with God, being half-hearted is worse than making no commitment. This attitude leads a candidate to a false assumption of salvation. Look at your motives to see if you have truly given your whole heart to Jesus. Do you see your faith as vibrant or just so, so? Don't fool yourself, for you're not fooling Jesus. Remember a whole heart cannot be a divided heart simultaneously. Do you find yourself serving the Lord half- heartedly? Do you go to church on Sunday and curse on your job on Monday? What should you do to change that in your life? First, look at your conversion. Did you honestly commit? Second, are you willing to repent and relinquish your control and give the Lord your whole heart now? Believing with your whole heart is the place to start in your walk with God. Trusting with your whole heart is next.

Prayer: Lord, in all I do please help me to do it with a whole heart. Replace my unbelief with a whole heart of acceptance and trust. In Your precious name, amen.

Personal Reflections: Are there times you find yourself being half-hearted in your belief and service? What one thing can you change to trust God more?

_____

_____

_____

_____

_____

_____

_____

_____

_____

_____

_____

_____

_____

_____

_____

_____

_____

_____

_____

_____

Re-writeable Heart (2 Corinthians 3:2-6)

"Being manifested that you are a letter of Christ cared for by us written not with ink, but with the Spirit of the living God, not on tablets of stone, but on <u>tablets of human hearts</u>."

I just bought a CD writer for my computer. I have learned that there are two types of disk that can be used on such a machine. One is writeable, and one is a re-writeable. That is, the first one can be only written on once and cannot be erased or re-recorded. The other one can be erased and used over and over. It is open to change. The same is so with man's heart. Some hearts are written on stone. It is hard, set in stone, it is not changeable. In the Bible, the stone is usually something that is permanent. But this passage gives us a different perspective. The Spirit writes his message now on our hearts. As free will humans, we have a choice either to let our hearts become stone or remain re-writeable. Even in our Christian lives we can allow our hearts to become hardened over time and not allow the Spirit to continue to rewrite our hearts according to His will. If we are willing to yield to the Spirit, then He will make our hearts new. God can erase the old information, ways, garbage, and put into our hearts the new message of life, of confidence, and a renewed ministry with His Spirit. Ask yourself if your heart is open to change, or you have been closing yourself to God's changing Word and Spirit? Are you willing to let Him cleanse you of your old outdated heart and renew it with His life-changing Spirit? We cannot do it alone, or on our own. God must do the rewrite, but we must do the yielding to His work in our lives. The same is with those who are making the decision to follow Jesus daily. Our commitment is to renew our heart not just accept Him as Savior. When there is no new heart, there is no new birth. Be encouraged that there is hope that God will re-write your heart.

Prayer: Lord, I open my heart to your Spirit to re-write on it as you wish. Help me to be open to your changing my life and heart. Lord, erase the negative information in my heart and replace it with your refreshing newness. Open my eyes and heart that I might see and be what you want me to be. In Jesus name I pray.

Personal Reflections: What can I do, or the local church do to be softer in heart? Are we doing enough?

_____

_____

_____

_____

_____

_____

_____

_____

_____

_____

_____

_____

_____

_____

_____

_____

_____

_____

_____

_____

_____

_____

_____

Soft Heart Deuteronomy 15:7

"If there is a poor man with you, one of your brothers, in any of your towns in your land which the Lord your God is giving you, you shall not harden your heart nor close your hand from your poor brother."

What does it mean, "not to harden your heart from your poor brother?" It means you allow yourself to be soft or compassionate of heart for those who are poor among you. What are the implications of this in the church, in your life, or in mine? I struggle with this. When I see a person on the side of the road begging, I want to look away. I have a mistrust of that person's motives. When I hear of those who are third generation welfare recipients, I sometime hold contempt for them because they are able bodied and capable of self-reliance. There are charlatans out there, and I have been used or burned before in giving to them. I have decided that if I give from the heart, then if they are using me, then God will deal with them in the end. Jesus said the poor would always be in our midst. That does not give us an excuse not to care. The word tells us not to close our hand from them. Do you have compassion for those in need? I must realize that I am one step from being poor. One step from losing all and immediately becoming poor. But I am not a person with a poor mentality. Some will be poor because they either have no will to get out of their situation, they are mentally challenged or they are ignorant of how to come out of their situation. Some are poor at anyone point in time, but they will not stay there if they have help, time, and resources to get out of their situation. Moses is talking to the people of God to take care of their own. There should be no one in the church on welfare if they are poor in deed. The word also says, "if you do not work you do not eat." This tells people, if you can work, then you should not be on welfare. The church should help people get a lift out of poverty. We should not be used, but we also should not turn our back on those in need, for someday we may need compassion too.

Prayer: Dear Father, please help me to see the poor around me and give me a soft/compassionate heart towards them.

Personal Reflections: When was the last time you helped someone in need? When did you refuse to help? Have you ever had to ask for help? Think of someone who may need your help. Pray for them then help them.

_____

_____

_____

_____

_____

_____

_____

_____

_____

_____

_____

_____

_____

_____

_____

Trembling Heart! (1 Samuel 4:13)
"There was Eli sitting on a seat by the wayside watching, for his heart trembled for the ark of God."

Have you ever had a trembling in your heart when the glory of God has been triumphal or maligned? Does your heart quake when people disregard, or put down your God and His servants, or has your heart gone numb in this world of compromise and disingenuity? Eli was a servant who had awe in his heart for the presence of God. When we realize who God is, we too should tremble with awe, respect, and fear. Let us not forget that we have that Shikina glory in us through His Spirit. Let us not allow the bombarding society and media to make us desensitized to His glory and awesomeness. It should never be that in your life, that you are called "Ichabod," that is, the glory of God has departed. Living under grace should not take away respect, awe, and a trembling heart. Rather, it should create it even more to know that His grace is found in our trembling and awe of His greatness and power. Also important is when we sin ourselves. Do we have a trembling heart when we sin? Some say we do not have to have trembling or contrite heart to be saved and should have no fear of our sins now. I disagree. When we lose any sense of fear or trepidation when we sin, then we can become numb to the effects of sin. Sin can get a foothold in our lives, and we may be stepping into the slippery slope of apostasy. Never trivialize your sins and shortcomings because the consequences may produce a nominal or lukewarm faith. A trembling heart due to sin can lead us to the point where we always are confessing our sins, for He is always cleansing us from those sins. More important, God would rather us tremble because we recognize who He is, and what it means to be in His presence. Christ gives us that opportunity to be in His presence.

Prayer: Lord, help me not to let your glory depart in my life. Help me to be so insensitive when your glory is compromised that my heart will fail to tremble. How long will you strive with a people that do not give you glory and tremble in your presence, not out of fear, but awe and respect?

Personal Reflections: What things should you tremble about today in a society void of God? List some sins that you might need to tremble about in your life. Then confess them. See 1 John 1

_____

_____

_____

_____

_____

_____

_____

_____

_____

_____

_____

_____

_____

_____

_____

_____

_____

_____

Troubled/convicted Heart (2 Samuel 24:10)

"And David's heart troubled him after he numbered the people. And David said I have sinned greatly… Oh Lord take away the iniquity of thy servant, for I have done very foolishly."

It does not matter what sin David committed this time. What matters is that he had a troubled heart about his sinning. It should never happen in one's lives that your walk with Christ comes to the point when you sin that you do not have a troubled heart. The first step to apostasy is our untroubled heart about our sin. An untroubled heart causes our soul to become callous to sin and, therefore, allows sin to reign in our daily lives. David had a troubled or remorseful heart in regard to his sin, and this led to repentance. It then becomes double sin when you do not have trouble with your sin and transgressions. The heart that is not troubled by the sin in the world will not be concerned about evangelism and concern for their souls. Furthermore, the heart that is not troubled with sin is also in trouble of losing or not having a relationship with God. God will not dwell with continual sin in one's life or camp. You see this every time in the Old Testament when the Israelites <u>totally</u> turned away from God, then God at times turned away from them. But we are under grace. Yes, but that does not give us a license to continually sin and not be remorseful about it. We though, unlike David, have the indwelling of the Holy Spirit to help us and convict us of sin daily, but we can resist Him and eventually quench Him in our lives. David sinned, but his heart was after Gods's heart. What this means is that he sinned, but his heart was a heart that did not want to sin, but rather have a deep relationship with God was his intent. If your heart is after Gods' then you too will have no problem in being sensitive and repentant of your sins. David saw that what he did was foolish, and he felt guilty. Guilt like this is what God is looking for in your heart.

Prayer: Lord, help me never to be callous and not have a troubled heart about sin. Through Your Spirit, trouble my heart and help me resist the temptation to look the other way and ignore my sin. Lord you are my refuge. Let me see you in the cleft of the rock, Amen,

Personal Reflections: What sins have not troubled you? Why? What should you do about it?

_____

_____

_____

_____

_____

_____

_____

_____

_____

_____

_____

_____

_____

_____

_____

_____

_____

_____

_____

_____

_____

_____

Understanding Heart (1 Kings 3:9-14)

"Therefore give to your servant an understanding heart....The speech pleased the Lord that Solomon had asked this thing."

How wonderful is it to please God? How many of our choices each day pleases the Lord? Have you asked for things that are selfish, or altruistic? As a young man, Solomon asked God for an understanding heart. To choose to understand the difference between good and evil is the basis for a righteous life. Understanding what the breadth, depth and height of who God is is should be the basis of our life long search. I am sure that back then, as now, the Holy Spirit gave Solomon his understanding and wisdom as He does to those who follow Him today. If he had asked for money, fame, or length of life, then God may have given those to him as well, but maybe without the wisdom and understanding to live it abundantly. Let us become like the young Solomon and ask for the things that make a difference in this life, and that please God. Jesus said to ask and knock, and it would be given, especially something that is dear to God's heart. Although Solomon asked for understanding, he did not always follow wise choices. But if we can start with understanding then we can know better what to do at any given moment in the wisdom and power of the Spirit. Have you ever found yourself understanding something or being enlightened on a subject or life issue, but still chose to go in the opposite direction? I guess we all have. Understanding is only an opportunity to do the right thing. If an understanding heart is void of faith or faith is given up, then you will suffer the consequences as Solomon did. Choose this day whom you will serve. The difference between Solomon and us today was that Solomon did not have the indwelling of the Holy Spirit, and we do if we are baptized disciples. Acts 2:38 Today we have little excuse to live a wise Spirit-filled life with God.

Prayer: Search my heart and make it known unto me. Lord, please give me an understanding wise heart in my life. The lack of it has gotten me into trouble, so give me an understanding of evil and good in me that I may know what to do. Help me to resist the evil one. Also, help me understand more of Your love and character.

Personal Reflections: Lord, have I asked and sought for things that pleases you or disappoints you? List both below and pray about what you should do with both.

_____

_____

_____

_____

_____

_____

_____

_____

_____

_____

_____

_____

_____

_____

_____

_____

_____

_____

_____

_____

_____

_____

Devoted Heart (I Kings)

"Let your heart therefore be devoted (loyal) to the Lord our God, to walk in His statutes and keep his commandments, as at this day."

God desired that the children of Israel, His chosen, would have wholly devoted and loyal hearts toward Him. Is this same request still valid from God? Does He still want Christians today to be concerned about these commitments since we are under grace? Being under grace does not eradicate our devotion or responsibility to follow Him and his commands. God has not changed His desire for us to be devoted in this way. Being wholly devoted hearts, means you cannot be lukewarm or cold to God. It means you have no problems with allegiance to God and the forsaking of all others. But unfortunately, they many times were not loyal to God, and this broke His heart. If your heart is totally and wholly devoted, then you will obey His commands. No less should we as children of God born under a new covenant. It is evident in I Kings that God did not set down a bunch of commands for the people to drudge through, but that people would totally commit to it out of a wholly devoted, unwavering heart, not part, but all in dedication to God. Jesus said, "if you love me you will obey my commandments." Is this just a request for us His disciples? I think not. His grace saves you, but will He save us if we do not love Him? NO. Therefore, if we are not concerned about obeying His two commandments of love, then are we truly His Saved Servant? Just think about it. The main thing that tears apart a marriage, or any relationship, is that they are not totally devoted and loyal to one another. God wants that same devotion, or there can never be the loyalty that binds. Some will say, "Were saved by grace, so we do not have to walk in His statutes." But does God want to give grace to someone who does not want to devote their life to Him? It is not about saying I believe, it is about having a relationship with God, any less and you might be fooling yourself for eternity.

Prayer: Help me Lord to be wholly devoted in my heart to you in everything'. Help me not to be a wavering or lukewarm half devoted child, but wholly devoted towards you and your will daily. In Your strength, amen.

Personal Reflections: Write the commands you find burdensome? What commands do you find a pleasure in your walk?

_____

_____

_____

_____

_____

_____

_____

_____

_____

_____

_____

_____

_____

_____

_____

_____

_____

_____

_____

_____

_____

Undevoted Heart (I Kings 15:3)

"And he walked in all the sins of his father which he had committed to him, and his heart was not wholly devoted to the Lord his God, like the heart of his father, David."

The saying "like father like son, does not always play out. It seems here that both father and son had their sins, but unlike David his grandfather Abijam did not have a heart that was devoted to God. One could interpret this to say that David did not have a devoted heart. I think the comparison is that David had one while his Son did not, because God Himself said David was after His own heart. Let us look at ourselves; we all sin even after we have committed to following Jesus as His disciple. But it is what lies in the heart that counts. A devoted heart is a true heart that ties itself to the one who is the object of the devotion. People who have a heart is one who is convicted of their sin because they have so much love and devotion that they do not want to hurt the one they are devoted to. That is; they do not want to hurt that person by sinning. But a person with a non-devoted heart does not care about their sin against the person and cannot be devoted because of their lack of care by sinning. Ask yourself when you sin, how do you feel? Do you feel sick about it? Do you feel remorse about your sin? If not, then your devotion needs to be questioned because you should have repented of your past and future sins. The commitment you should have to God is that you will try to not sin in the future. The devoted person will begin to sin less and less because of their devotion. What things are you devoted to or give your time to each day? Your devotion will tell you, and others who is the apple of your eye. If it is the pleasures of the world then your sins will find you, and you will not be devoted to Jesus as Lord. So ask yourself if you're devoted to God, or do you still live like you did before you gave your life to God? If there has been no change then you may not be devoted to God and your sins will find you out.

Prayer: Lord, help me -to lose my devotion to you. Lord, help my devotion for I know I am not as devoted as I should be. Help me to sin less so that I will wholly devote my heart to you, oh Lord.

Personal Reflections: Are there any things in your life that is not devoted to God? What can you do to be devoted?

_____

_____

_____

_____

_____

_____

_____

_____

_____

_____

_____

_____

_____

_____

_____

_____

_____

_____

_____

_____

_____

_____

_____

_____

Joyful, Glad Heart (I Kings 8:66)

"On the eighth day he sent the people away: and they blessed the king and went to their tents joyful and glad of heart for all the good that the Lord had done for His servant David and Israel, His people."

Think back to times when your heart was joyful and glad. It may be today, at this moment, or at least yesterday. Think of times when you were glad of heart, and what caused that joy? The people were glad at what the Lord had blessed them with that day. Can you recall in your spiritual life when there was joy? Can you remember where God has blessed you and your fellow believers? If not, then maybe you have not been looking. Joy is a choice and a frame of mind. I have seen people who should have had a joyful heart for what has happened in their life, but they seem to look at the cup half empty. Something is always wrong or going bad. The people chose this way of life, the way they framed their reality, but it should not have been their reality. Think of the blessings in your life and let yourself rejoice for what God has done. It is easy to be joyful over some human victor or sports team, so why not in our spiritual life? No matter what happens in the day- to-day journey, we must keep sight that with Christ we have victory even when we seem to be in defeat. Rejoice in the Lord always. How can we do this? As disciples/believers, we can look to another realm and know that if we are in His will we will be blessed eternally. Even now we can thank Him for even our trials for in them we are being made whole, and a better person. Things can always be worse. Let us look at all our blessings now, and what's to become. Don't forget the idea, "I complained once about the holes in my shoes until I met a man who had no feet." There is always someone worse off than you, but the main point is that no matter what the circumstance, we can have joy in the Lord.

Prayer: Lord, let me not be inhibited of bursting forth with a glad heart for who you are and for what you have done for me. Forgive me when I fail to praise you and choose to be joyful and glad of heart. Help me to be more joyful about your victory in every day, now and forever.

Personal Reflections: Find a joyful song and sing it. Think of a sad time and find some joy in it.

_____

_____

_____

_____

_____

_____

_____

_____

_____

_____

_____

_____

_____

_____

_____

_____

_____

_____

_____

_____

_____

_____

_____

Wayward Heart (I Kings 11:1-4)

"From the nations of whom the Lord had said to the Children of Israel, "You shall not intermarry with them, nor they with you, Surely, they will turn away your hearts after their gods. Solomon clung to these in love."

Just like life, the Bible is full of both the joys and sadness. God recorded for our events and people's lives so that those coming afterward might learn and not go down the same dark path. Here we have Solomon, the wisest man in the world, brought down by foolish disobedience. God commanded that the children of Israel not marry others from other nations, for He knew that they would cause them to turn away from the one true God to idols. Solomon put himself in a situation that led his heart to turn away from God. One cannot serve two masters, and neither could the wisest man. When we disobey and put ourselves in places with certain people, the result will be the same. Let us be careful lest we become too proud and say, "Oh it won't get bother me I can do this or that." But if you play with fire long enough, you will get burned. Focus on the things above and put off those things of the world. Do not be unequally yoked in marriage, or in friendship or your heart may be led away. Paul struggled with this issue when he said that he struggled to do what he knows is right. What are we to do? First, stay clear of those who may tempt you to go their way. Association does not mean that you do not associate with others to win them to Christ, but you must not be their associates in sin. The most important factor is your devotion and commitment to God. If it is weak, then you will be easy prey for others to lead you astray. Remember, "Greater is the one who is in you than he that is in the world." Philippians 4 God is a jealous God, and He wants our total love. Who is your first love? Giving God total love is hard for each of us to be faithful, but we must make it our quest to do so even if we find it difficult.

Prayer: Lord, help me not to have a wayward heart. Lord give me your Spirit, lead me to those for whom I can be a light and the wisdom to run away from those who will destroy me and turn me away from God. Let me be like David in the area of faithfulness and follow the Lord till the end.

Personal Reflections: What people or circumstances are there in your life that may turn your heart away from God? What must you do to protect your faith, but at the same time be salt and light?

_____

_____

_____

_____

_____

_____

_____

_____

_____

_____

_____

_____

_____

_____

_____

_____

_____

_____

_____

_____

_____

_____

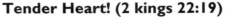

Tender Heart! (2 kings 22:19)

"Because your heart was tender, and you humbled yourself before the Lord when you heard what I spoke against this place and against its inhabitants."

Because the King had a tender heart towards God, God blessed him. What is a tender heart towards God? If it is the opposite of a hard heart, we might have a clue. The King's heart became tender or soft towards God. God was able to work with him, and he was open to God at this point. He became humble, not hardened, and proud as did many of the Israelites or even like Pharaoh. This tender or soft heart allowed the king to have a remorseful attitude about what was going to happen to him and his people. Do you have a tender/soft heart towards God and His will for your life? If you do, then you will be open to the next step, and that is a repentant heart. You cannot repent if you are not tender and humble in your heart. When you see others around you heading for destruction is your heart tender towards them or hardened? If it is tender then you will want to help them see God; if it heart is hardened, then you will not think or care about them. A true evangelist is one who has a tender heart towards those who are perishing. Compassion towards the poor and downtrodden is also a by-product of a tender heart. God will be as tender or soft towards you as you are with your relationship with Him and others. A tender heart is the beginning of love towards others, so have a tender heart that you may be open to God and His loving response to you. How can we get a tender heart but by being humble? When we are prideful, we tend to be unconcerned about others because our focus is on ourselves. Be like this king. Be tender and humble so that God will bless you and those around you. You will then find that when you do others will give you what you need.

Prayer: Lord, help my heart always to be tender towards you and your Word, as well as those around me. Open my heart and my eyes that I may see and not become hardened by the world and circumstances.

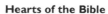

Personal Reflections: In what way have been hard-hearted towards God and others. When have I seen the truth of God's word and not been touched by its truth?

_____

_____

_____

_____

_____

_____

_____

_____

_____

_____

_____

_____

_____

_____

_____

_____

_____

_____

_____

_____

Faithful Heart (Nehemiah 9:5-8)

"You found his heart faithful before you and made a covenant with him."

Oh, how wonderful to be called a faithful one of God. My hope that in the future people will say of me, "He was faithful to God." Abraham was such a person. We can look at many examples of Job, David, and countless others, but what is important is what God will say to you and me. What does a faithful heart look like in God's eyes? It is a heart that stays true and dedicated no matter what is asked or put in front of us. It is a heart that believes that God will be there and see us through our troubles and daily life. It will be a heart that does not listen or follow other voices or temptations and lose faithfulness. A faithful heart is at the foundation of our journey. Without it, all the other aspects of the heart would be nullified. A faithful heart still follows when it seems there is no one to follow, or nowhere to go. Abraham did not see into his future, but he had faith that God would be glorified and would provide a way in every case. Today we must be found faithful. When we are, then God will give to the faithful in heart the promises with those He has made a covenant. The new covenant is based on our faithfulness to Jesus under His Lordship. To the faithful He will be faithful. Every covenant with God has been based upon the faith of the person who is the recipient of that covenant. Abraham and even the children of Israel were required to have faith to fulfill the covenant between them. The same is between us and God today. If we do not have saving faith and continued faithfulness, then God will not make a covenant with us. The covenant of Jesus as Lord of our lives, each day is what we are to strive for in our devotion to God. Faithfulness is not mere belief, but a committed faithful life that follows Jesus as Lord. Christ offers his covenant to each of us. It is up to each of us to be faithful to our part of the covenant.

Prayer: Lord, help me to be like Abraham, being faithful in heart. Lord, forgive me when my heart has failed this test. Lord, strengthen my heart by the power and presence of your Word and Spirit.

Personal Reflections: In what areas have you been faithful? What areas have you not been faithful? In the last question what can you do to be more faithful?

_____

_____

_____

_____

_____

_____

_____

_____

_____

_____

_____

_____

_____

_____

_____

_____

_____

_____

_____

_____

_____

_____

_____

Faint Heart (Job 23:9-17)

"For God made my heart faint (weak), and the almighty terrifies me." v.16

In this world where people strive for strength and power, it is not a positive outlook to be weak. But we are not to live in this world. For when we are weak we then put into perspective our relationship with God, or what should be our relationship or attitude. "I am weak but thou art strong." Unless we see this weak/strong relationship, we will never be able to allow the right relationship with God to develop. If we base or strength on God's Strength, then we will be able to grow and can stand when times are rough. Unfortunately, sometimes, God has to come to us or needs to make our heart weak so that in Him we can be strong. If we do not fear Him and we see ourselves as totally sufficient, then we will not come to Him as we should. Job knew his strength came from God. If we are to grow in Christ, we too must know where our true strength should come from to be overcomers. Any other source and we are fooling ourselves and truly will be weak of heart in times of darkness and need. Fear is the beginning of wisdom. It is also true that a healthy fear of who God is should make us weak in His presence. We do have the promises that if we are in Christ, our fears are subdued because of His love for us. But what should we do about being terrified of the unknown or the future? Should we? Or should we shun this idea in the presence of a loving God? Job, of course, had a lot of experiences that none of us want to experience, but his heart attitude we must immolate when we come into His presence each day. Therefore, come before the Lord with humility knowing that it is in God, through Jesus, that we have a weak heart in perspective of our need. Let Him lift us up and give us His strength. In our weakness is His power.

Prayer: Lord, I realize that you are my strength and that in and of myself I can do nothing. Lord, if I am being self-sufficient to the point of being unfaithful then help me to be weak in your sight so that you can truly make me strong. In Your lovely hands, I give myself, amen.

Personal Reflections: In what areas do you consider yourself self-sufficient? When have you seen times where you were weak, and you needed God's strength? How can you be weak while letting God be strong in your life?

_____

_____

_____

_____

_____

_____

_____

_____

_____

_____

_____

_____

_____

_____

_____

_____

_____

_____

_____

_____

Uprightness in heart (Ps 7:10; 64:10; 94:15)
"For judgment will again be righteous, and all the upright in heart will follow it." 94:15

When you read each passage about the upright heart in each context, it is obvious either man's righteousness or God's righteousness is mentioned. God is righteous, and He tests the hearts and minds of each of us to see if our hearts are upright or down right dirty. The upright heart does right things. The upright will stand up in their life and others for what is right. Being righteous is practicing right things. It is becoming righteous in thought and deed. An upright heart is one that rejoices in doing what is right. The passage says that being upright in heart will be the salvation for us, and God will protect us and be our shield. To be upright is practical both now and in eternity. If our heart is not upright, then we are planning our demise. Our non-upright heart or deeds we choose to do will come back to punish us here and now. Consequences of our actions or non-upright acts will not fall under God's protection. If He has made us holy, then let us be holy in life. In Ephesians, we are encouraged to put on the Breastplate of righteousness. Whose plate is it? It is Christ. To put this plate on means, we act like Christ. We are to try to live like he would live in doing so we will protect ourselves. If we are upright, we will follow the judgments of God. We will see that what He does will be worth following. He is not just suggesting that we put it on, but He expects us to, for our safety from the evil one. Let us be practical. What local laws or statutes have you ignored and trivialized? Have you ever gone over the speed limit? The traffic cops usually only stop you if you're more than 10 miles over. Now I am stepping on my toes, and I do not like it. How about you? Will you be upright in heart and follow even when no one is looking?

Prayer: Lord, as a man I find that it is not always easy to do right things and resist evil ways. Help me to yield my heart and ways to the power of your Spirit. Teach me and shield me in your righteousness. I know the righteousness of Christ saves me, but Lord, I know I too need to be right in the heart. I pray this in your Name, Amen.

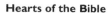

Personal Reflections: Think of at least one act of uprightness you did this week. Think of two or more you might have next week.

_____

_____

_____

_____

_____

_____

_____

_____

_____

_____

_____

_____

_____

_____

_____

_____

_____

_____

_____

_____

_____

_____

Pure Heart (Ps 51:10, 11 Matthew 5:8)
"Who may ascend the hill of the Lord? Who can stand in His holy place? The pure in heart shall see God."

Where is His hill, His holy place, and what does it mean to be pure in heart? It is obvious that God is holy and pure and that to be in His presence we too must be pure. When we make this stand with God by being pure, then we can see God face to face. Moses was on such a hill and holy place, and he did see a slight part of God. What a thrill that must have been, but today we can begin to see God, to come into his holy place spiritually. We can come into His place when we come before Him by being purified by following Jesus and being purified by His Spirit. Those who cleanse their hands and purify their hearts can begin to understand and see God for who He is. A pure heart is a genuine heart, a heart that is pure from, and clean of selfish motives. It is a heart much like a child's open and honest. If our hearts are not pure then that which makes it impure will get in the way or cloud our view of God. God will not honor or open His holy place to those who are not. To begin we must humbly pray "Create in me a clean, pure heart, oh God, and renew a steadfast spirit within me." If the presence of God is the place you want to end up, then now is the time to let Him purify your heart. His hill today is everywhere a heart is pure and clean before Him. The more we are pure, the more we will see Him. How do you become pure? Get rid of the impure things in your life. What are they? Look at His word and begin there. Remember it always starts with your will to be pure and then you're yielding to the Holy Spirit to do the work in your heart. No one has the power or means to make their heart pure unless they allow God through the Spirit to do the work. It is a partnership where you must be willing to cease from an impure lifestyle, both in thought and action.

Prayer: Oh Lord, search me and reveal to me any impurity in my heart. Help me to cleanse my heart and hands, so that I can be pleasing in your sight. Oh Lord, you are greatly to be praised. Let me be in your presence; purify my heart in your sight. In your precious name.

Personal Reflections: What do I have to do, or change to purify my heart?

_____

_____

_____

_____

_____

_____

_____

_____

_____

_____

_____

_____

_____

_____

_____

_____

_____

_____

_____

_____

_____

Desiring/Craving Heart!! (Psalm 10:3)
"For the wicked boast of his heart's desire, and the greedy man curses and spurns the Lord.

We all have desires, dreams and urges that move us to act, become and behave as we do. Desire is a root of or cause of, our wants and wishes in life. How does this affect a person's walk with God? The man who allows his raw desires allows them to become his god. It is easy to become greedy or overcome by our desires so that we are self-centered and self-absorbed in the pleasure of our desires. Our pleasures become our focus and our god. This type of person spurns or pushes God aside. There is no God he confesses, for not to do so might require him to give up some of his wicked desires. It is obvious that a wicked heart will have wicked desires. God wants us to desire from a humble upright heart. When your heart is God-centered, then you will have Godly desires. One of my biggest desires is to see people grow and watch the light go on in their minds when I teach them some truth from the Bible. Oh, what a joy. If your desires are holy, then the more God will hear you, and strengthen you, and your joy will be God's desire. Wickedness and desire for God are opposites and truly cannot come out of a person who desires God. What is your heart's desire? Is it wicked, or is it godly? If you are trying to follow the Lord, then make your heart desire His desire. How do you do this? You must know what He desires. The Bible is the place you must go to find out those desires. You also must take control of your desires that are wicked and replace them with God's. Be careful, for what you desire, you may get it. The wicked desire evil because they are selfish as we were once when we were not in Christ. Where your desire is shown where your love is. Where is your heart?

Prayer: Lord, it is a battle to keep the desires of the flesh under control, so strengthen my heart to desire Godly things, ways, and thoughts. Lord, teach me your way and help me to die to self in the areas of my desires that may lead to control by the flesh. Help me desire godly desires so that I do not spurn you, my God. I pray this in your precious name, Amen.

Personal Reflections: What do you boast about in your life? Which of your desires are wicked, and which ones are God's desires?

_____

_____

_____

_____

_____

_____

_____

_____

_____

_____

_____

_____

_____

_____

_____

_____

_____

_____

_____

_____

_____

Broken hearted (Psalm 34:18; 51:17)

"The Lord is near to the brokenhearted and saves those who are crushed in spirit."

Should a Christian who is saved by grace and who is told to rejoice always also be brokenhearted and crushed in spirit? This psalm says that God is near and saves the brokenhearted. I think God still is near concerns Himself with the broken hearted. For it takes a broken heart to come to God in the first place. The person who needs Christ in his life must come to him with a broken heart. However, this goes against modern day evangelism of "woo them with the free grace and benefits of salvation." Be careful not to scare them away by all this broken stuff, we need to lift people up. But has God changed His likes and dislikes from the Old Testament to the New Testament? I think not. We are to rejoice that gave us such woedrful grace. That is why more when we fail Him and do not walk in His ways, we should react with a broken heart. We should be broken hearted when we sin, we truly cannot come to God and be in His presence. When times we are broken hearted and remorseful that we can feel the hand of God, and His healing forgiving heart. Being a person of grace, you must receive that grace with a broken heart. To have the Holy Spirit be able to fill you and work for you, you must first be crushed or broken in your spirit to allow Him room to come in and fill you. To be near the Lord, you first must be broken hearted. In these acts, the Lord will save. The Bible also says that we must repent before God will save us. One cannot repent if he does not have a broken or remorseful heart first. Rejoice, and again I say rejoice because our broken heart is healed by His salvation and grace. Jesus, our healer, has mended our broken hearts. Let Him now begin that healing in you.

Prayer: Oh Lord show me the ways I break your heart. Help me never to go through life and not be brokenhearted about my sin. Heal me, and I will rejoice in my need of you. I rejoice that you do heal, and you do listen to us who are broken hearted. Thank you for lifting us up, for a broken heart is only for a season, rejoicing is for eternity. I pray this in your precious name. Amen.

Personal Reflections: Remember the last time you were broken hearted. How did you feel God's presence? What did He do to mend it?

_____

_____

_____

_____

_____

_____

_____

_____

_____

_____

_____

_____

_____

_____

_____

_____

_____

Happy heart (Proverbs 15:13)

"A joyful/happy heart makes a cheerful face, but when the heart is sad, the spirit is broken."

Now we are going to focus on the happy or joyful heart. It has been said that it takes more muscles to deal with a frown than a smile. When you see another person smile at you, how does it make you feel? Can you resist smiling when someone smiles at you? Can you abstain from laughing when someone laughs? It is just contagious. You must force yourself not to smile or laugh. What does a smile on your face do for you? When I smile or laugh, there is a sense of euphoria, a change of feeling in our minds and hearts. But the cheerful face must be preceded by a happy heart. Where does this heart come from? Does everything have to be in order or going your way for you to be happy? Well, it helps, I would think. But some have said that happiness is a state of mind about the way you view life. When it rains on your parade, can you be happy for the good the rain will bring, or is everything gloom and doom? For some people, gloom and doom are the clouds that hover over them, and they would be disappointed if it were not there to complain about. God wants His children to have a smile on their faces due to their happy, motivated heart. Think when you smiled at something. What was it that made you smile? It was something that made you happy or joyful in your heart. It may have been some kind word, some dream come true, or maybe you made someone else happy and it rubbed off on you too. That is what God wants for you. In turn how do others feel when you smile at them? Is that not your gift for them, yourself, and God? The greatest thing that should make us happy and cheerful of face is that our Lord loved us enough to come to this earth and call us his children. The saddest face is a believer that fails to think, be happy, and smile due to God's blessings and grace. So, face and heart, get it together and smile.

Prayer: Lord, help my heart to smile. Help my face to show my joy and happiness to others and you. Forgive me when I allow my "stinking thinking" to put a frown on my face. In your precious name.

Personal Reflections: List some things that make you smile. Also, make a list of those things that rob you of happiness. Focus then on the first and try to overcome the later.

_____

_____

_____

_____

_____

_____

_____

_____

_____

_____

_____

_____

_____

_____

_____

_____

_____

_____

_____

_____

Sad Heart Proverbs 15:13

"A joyful/happy heart makes a cheerful face, but when the heart is sad, the spirit is broken."

The opposite of the happy heart is the sad one. Being happy and having a good outlook on life will bring blessings of health to your body and relationships. The sad heart produces negative results to all aspects of your life. What does a sad face reveal about a person? What a person's face shows is usually based on what is in a person's heart. Yes, a person can fake a smile now and then, but the genuine heart will come forth sooner or later when the person's guard is down. The sadness is more than skin deep and smiles on your face. The heart is the seat of our soul and the base of what, and who we are. What does it mean to have a sad heart? There are as many reasons as there are people. Usually, people have valid reasons for being sad. Things happen in our broken world with broken people. We all have broken pieces in our lives due to death, sickness, accidents, and relationships that are toxic and sour. How a person deals with this brokenness will determine the lasting effect on the heart and wellbeing of that person. There are results of having a sad heart. A broken spirit is one. What are the implications of a broken spirit? A person can have a sad heart, and it takes time for each of us to deal with that sadness. When a person lets the sadness continue to grow and continue in their heart, then they will develop a broken spirit. Again, this broken spirit can be for a time, or it can linger to the point that the person cannot function, and in some cases gives up. It is not a sin to have a sad heart or broken spirit over something in your life. The concern is when this sadness rules your life, and you cannot cope. When this happens, a person of faith is not living a victorious life in Christ. Rejoice, and again I say rejoice, even in your sadness. I know while you're in this state of sadness this can sound trite, but it is during this time that you and I need God most.

Prayers: Father, I know I will have sadness and brokeness in my life. These are the times when I need you most. I realize that you are with me and will never forsake me. So, turn my sadness into joy.

Personal Reflections: What makes your heart sad? When have you felt your spirit was broken? What do you do or who do you go to when you are sad and broken?

_____

_____

_____

_____

_____

_____

_____

_____

_____

_____

_____

_____

_____

_____

_____

_____

_____

_____

_____

Steadfast heart! (Psalm 112:7)

"He will not fear evil tidings; His heart is steadfast, trusting in the Lord."

You cannot turn on the TV or read the newspaper, and not hear of evil tidings. What is the human norm? It is to fear, especially when we do not know what will happen in the future. What makes us uncomfortable or afraid when we hear evil news? In many cases, we have no control over the situation or news, so we seem to fear what we have no control over or understand. Therefore, the unknown is also debilitating and causes us to fear. This world has evil things at every turn. The Word says that the fear of the Lord is the beginning of wisdom. Those who trust in the Lord will only fear the Lord and not the evil tidings of the world. Where do we begin to trust in the Lord? The first thing is to see that God has ultimate control of the universe and the final events. When we trust in the Lord; we place ourselves in the hands of the Lord, and not the evil tidings or events. Therefore, even in the unknown results, or evil around us we can be steadfast, or firm in the heart, that all will work out for those who trust and depend on the Lord. What do you fear? Why do you fear? If so who do you trust? Your fears or the Lord? There is also the promise that, "greater is He that is in you, than he that is in the world." Who is at the source of evil tidings? Yes, the adversary himself. Your heart will be wavering if you allow Satan and your fears to control you. Remember, the only way your heart can be steadfast is because you have daily trusted in the Lord as His disciple. What good is it to trust today and be afraid tomorrow? I know who holds tomorrow, and, therefore, my heart is steadfast in Jesus my Lord. My heart will not move, because I have faith that He will not move from me.

Prayer: Lord, help me to trust in you when all around me there are evil events and news that are negative and scary. Lord, help my heart to be firm and steadfast in your hands. Help me to trust you and not my fears. Lord, help my unbelief and give me a heart that is steadfast and strong. In His name, Amen

Personal Reflections: What things in your life cause you to fear? How can you become more steadfast in heart towards God?

_____

_____

_____

_____

_____

_____

_____

_____

_____

_____

_____

_____

_____

_____

_____

_____

_____

_____

_____

Secure/upheld heart (Psalm 112:8)

"His heart is upheld/secure, he will not fear until he looks with satisfaction on his adversaries."

Have you ever faced an enemy or adversary? I have, and unless you have been on a deserted island all your life then you have too. You probably had a number of kinds of feelings about the altercation. You may have felt a sense of confidence if you were bigger or confident you could win. You may have felt afraid because of the unknown, or because the adversary was stronger than you. You may have felt indifferent or not interested in making the fight. But how do you feel when you win? I have been in a lot of adversarial battles especially in the sports world. It is a great feeling when you are victorious over your competition. When you lose, it is sad feeling. In the spiritual realm who are our adversaries or foes? We can start with the great adversary, Satan. He is out to make us fear; he is out to defeat us and make our hearts insecure. So, who secures our heart? Who upholds it against any adversary? It is our Lord; and our relationship with Jesus that makes our heart secure. Why? Because it is only in Christ that we can be victorious. Because He was victorious over His and our adversary death, and it's author the devil, we too can be victorious. This then gives us a satisfaction that we are upheld by Him. We must remember the verse, "Greater is He that is in us than he that is in the world." This verse should give you security in your life because believing so is real life, real power, and real security for the believer. If you will only believe it and allow the Spirit to give you security. Why is there satisfaction in overcoming your fears and your adversaries? First, God is glorified for holding you up, and you who call upon the Lord will be called faithful or trusting Him with your fears. What are the fears that control you? Yield to the one who can give you the security over your adversaries and free you from fear.

Prayer: Lord, you alone can secure or uphold our heart when we go against our adversary. Lord we need your help to defeat the adversary in our lives. Help us not to fear, for greater are you that are in us. Thank You, Lord.

Personal Reflections: What adversaries are in your life? Do you feel secure in your relationship with the Lord? List the adversaries that you need to overcome.

_____

_____

_____

_____

_____

_____

_____

_____

_____

_____

_____

_____

_____

_____

_____

_____

_____

_____

Embittered Heart (Psalm 73:21-24)

"When my heart was embittered, and I was pierced within. What does it take to pierce you to the core? What does it take to grieve your heart to the point of being embittered? What makes you angry? When a person is embittered about something which is hurt the most? Usually, the person that is embittered is hurt more than the object. What does bitterness do to a person? Medically defined, bitterness held within is an utterly devastating thing for a person's soul, body, and well-being. When you are bitter, all kinds of things happen to you physically and mentally. The longer you hold it in, the worse it becomes for you. Bitterness can affect your total system and tear down your immune system causing many types of illnesses. When the scripture says, "I was pierced within" the Bible was describing the effects of bitterness on a person. In most cases, the one you are bitter towards is not as affected as you are. Usually they are not aware of the bitterness or have already dealt with the problem. You must ask who is in control of your bitterness. When you allow your thoughts and anger to control you, then it controls you from head to toe. Your whole body is at risk when you let the bitterness control you. How do you overcome this bitterness that pierces your soul? How can you be healed? You will not be healed until you do two things. First, Go to God and let Him know about your struggles and need to have Him heal you from the inside through the Spirit's power. Second, deal with those you are bitter towards. It does not matter who is at fault go and reconcile. If they do not want to reconcile, then you have tried. Let it not destroy you. Take your thoughts captive and do not let them overwhelm you. It is hard for our flesh for we want to fight back and hurt those who hurt us. But this will only hurt you more, and continue the bitterness between you, and you will lose in the end. Forgiveness is your only way to conquer your bitter heart.

Prayer: Lord, help my bitterness. Help me to forgive those whom I have bitterness towards. Also, Lord, help me take control of my thoughts and feelings so that I may deal with my bitterness and be healed by You. Thank you for your forgiveness. In Jesus name, Amen.

Personal Reflections: List at least two events or persons that have embittered you. Then think of a way to overcome that bitterness.

_____

_____

_____

_____

_____

_____

_____

_____

_____

_____

_____

_____

_____

_____

_____

_____

_____

_____

_____

_____

_____

_____

Enlarged Heart (Psalm 119:32)
"I shall run the way of thy commandments for thou will enlarge my heart."

Can you put the same amount of liquid in a pint that you can a quart? Of course not, that is impossible. Can you put more wisdom and love in a closed heart or mind? Of course, not when you are closed to God's instructions. If one is not open to allowing new thoughts or ideas in, then it will not happen; no change will take place. The psalmist tells that when one runs or lives within the confines of God's commandments then one's heart will be enlarged. The more we allow God to teach us, and put His word in us, then our hearts and minds will be enlarged. When you stretch something pliable, you make way for more volume to come into the container. On the other hand, if we close our heart, then our heart will become hard and eventually break apart. We determine how large our heart or mind will become. Each person who decides will follow God's commandments and allow God to enlarge their heart. When you became a believer, what did you know about God? Can you remember how much maturity you had? Fast forward to now and look into your heart. Have you changed? Have you grown in knowledge and spiritual disciplines, or are you still where you were? If you are still where you were when you first believed, then you have not allowed God to enlarge your capacity to know Him and become more like Him. We see that God enlarged Solomon's mind/heart to take on more of God's wisdom because he asked for it. (1Kings 4:29). This same request is for everyone of us no matter how long we have been a believer, or how old we think we are. If we cease to allow God to pour His wisdom into us then we cease growing, and God just might as well take us home with Him if He cannot enlarge our hearts anymore.

Prayer: Lord, please enlarge my heart each day. Help me to let more of you into my mind, to expand it, to teach me your ways. Let me run in your steps and not in my way. Lord, forgive me for the times I have run away, for the times I have closed my heart to your teachings and wisdom. I pray this in your precious name, amen.

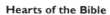

Personal Reflections: What things do you need changed in your life to enlarge your heart/mind?

_____

_____

_____

_____

_____

_____

_____

_____

_____

_____

_____

_____

_____

_____

_____

_____

_____

_____

_____

Open heart (Psalm 139:23,24)

"Search me O God and know my heart, try me and know my anxious thoughts. And see if there is any hurtful (evil) way within me."

Transparency is a key word today. Everyone that wants someone to be honest when they say, "What we need from you is transparency. That is, we need you to be honest and totally open with us." What God wants most from us is that we have this transparent attitude with Him. Does God need us to be transparent for Him to know who we are? I think not, because He knows all and sees all. What is transparency all about? It is about our becoming transparent to ourselves. When we say, "Search me O God," then two things happen. First, we show God our humbleness by being open to His searching of our whole being. This attitude opens up His love towards us. Second, we open our minds and hearts up to the windows of our soul, mind, and spirit. When we do this, we begin to see our true selves, and as well begin the road to healing and transformation. But what do we usually do? We try to rationalize and convince ourselves we're ok or try to suppress our thoughts spiritually. When we allow God to search us, He opens up our hearts and minds to really understand and know ourselves so that we can begin to make the changes we need to and think differently overcoming our anxious thoughts. We are anxious because of not dealing with our evil ways and thoughts. When we give God permission to search us and open us up to honesty, we begin to change. What things do you tend to want to hide or rationalize from God and yourself? Each of us needs to be open to knowing any evil thing in us so that we can change. You have two choices, search yourself or blind yourself to the truth. You choose. Your choice will determine your closeness with God. The benefits you will gain for your honesty is healing from your anxiety and your faith will grow.

Prayer: Lord search my heart, let me know if there is any hurtful or evil ways in me help me to deal with each one, as well with my anxious thoughts. Help me to take control of my thoughts and cleanse me from any evil ways or thoughts. I pray this in Your name.

Personal Reflections: List your anxious thoughts plus any hurtful things in your life. Then, think of ways to overcome them.

_____

_____

_____

_____

_____

_____

_____

_____

_____

_____

_____

_____

_____

_____

_____

_____

_____

_____

_____

_____

Mischief Heart (Psalm 140:2,3)
"Preserve me from violent men, who devise evil things in their hearts, they continually stir up wars."

The Hebrew Text uses "mischief in their hearts" instead of "devise evil." This sounds like the bullies I lived with during my grade school years. They seemed only to want to stir up trouble and do harm to weaker classmates. It seemed they had mischief in their heart. Sadly, little bullies grow up to be big bullies much of the time. My worst moments in life had been when so-called Christians devised evil towards me. They lied and tried to destroy what I was doing for the Lord. They seem to stir up wars or battles that wish to destroy others. Look at this world and see that evil men and women abide in this world, and they wish to do mischief. They desire to stir things to the point of destruction. The prayer here is to preserve me or protect me from evil, violent men even in the church. Does this always happen? Just because we are disciples does this mean we will be safe from the evil men of the world? There is no guarantee that we will always be protected. If you see how the disciples were treated, and how Christians over the years have been challenged or destroyed then one would wonder. But this does not or should not cause us not to pray for protection, especially in the spiritual realm. Be not concerned about those who can harm our body, but those who can harm the soul. In this, we can be hopeful when we hope in Christ through the power of the Holy Spirit. There will be war; there will be violent or mischief men and women in our lives, but we do not have to let them win by destroying us. Prayer is the key, and our faithfulness in the power of Christ who lives in us. We cannot do it alone, that is why we need the Spirit to overcome the mischief ones in our lives. The most important heart is ours. That is why we need to check our hearts daily to see that there is no mischief in our hearts.

Prayer: Lord, please protect me from violent men who want to destroy me. I know that they exist and help me to stand against the arrows of the evil one and his violent men. Help me to realize that this life is not all there is. I pray this in your precious name. Amen.

Personal Reflections: List some of those who have made mischief
your life. Pray to forgive them, and then do not let them control you
in your thoughts.

_____

_____

_____

_____

_____

_____

_____

_____

_____

_____

_____

_____

_____

_____

_____

_____

_____

Wise heart (Proverbs 10:8; Ecc. 8:5)

"The wise of heart will receive commands, but a babbling fool will be thrown down."

I remember when I was a child that my parents, especially my Dad, gave me a rule or command. If I wanted to know what fear Moses felt in the presence of God, I would think of my Dad when he gave me a command. Sometimes I would think, "Okay," this may be a good command and others I would think, what is he thinking of? There were, though, the consequences of talking back or disobeying Dad. It was not a wise thing. But I found out as I grew that most of His commands were good, and for my benefit, and always with good intention. The same is with God, except we know that God's commands are always perfect for us. A wise person will receive God's command with thanksgiving and obedience. Why is it wise to receive God's commands? Because He loves us and knows what is best; therefore, we would be foolish not to trust and obey God. We are a fool because of the consequences of not receiving His commands. First, we would be a fool because there are negative consequences to not receiving His commands. Some consequences bring bad results in this life and even possibly deadly ones for eternity. Second, is the consequence of not receiving all the blessings of following His commands? Is God going to ask us to eat a stone? No, his commands will be a blessing, even when we cannot see or feel them. Receive the blessings and don't be cast down. Those who are unwise in their hearts have a hard time a learning anything. They think they know it all and, therefore, will not listen to anyone, even though, the facts prove they are wrong. In most cases, their selfish agenda outweighs their wisdom, and stupidity takes over. But not those who follow Jesus and His commands. Those who have a new mind in Christ will gladly receive any command or instruction with joy, knowing that whatever God ask of us will be for our good.

Prayer: Lord, help me not to be a fool. Help me to be wise in my heart about the commands God has given me to follow Him, to love others, to do good, and not to do badly. Forgive me when I do not. Help me to know your commands and receive them with joy and obedience. I pray this in your precious name, Amen.

Personal Reflections: What commands do you have problems in following? Write down some blessings of following them and try to follow one each day this week.

_____

_____

_____

_____

_____

_____

_____

_____

_____

_____

_____

_____

_____

_____

_____

_____

_____

_____

_____

Anxious heart (Proverbs 12:25)

"Anxiety in the heart of a man weighs it down, but a good word makes it glad."

What an understatement: "anxiety weighs a man down." Much evidence today shows on how anxiety is harmful to our whole being. What does anxiety do, and why? How have you felt when you were in an anxious situation? Does your body get heavy, does it tingle? Do you feel out of control? What causes anxiety? Anxiety is often due to a number of factors like fear or uncontrollable situations that lead to a sense of not being in control. Is it a sin to be anxious because neither you nor God is in control? Are anxiousness and faith opposite? I have found myself anxious at times, and during these episodes, I remember trying to talk myself out of the feelings, trying to do things to relax my anxiousness through deep breathing and telling myself to calm down I can get through this. During these times I do feel a heaviness that seems overwhelming. What should you tell yourself when you go through this type of anxiety? If it is due to worry or stressful situations, then call upon the Lord to come to your side and ease your fears and uncertainty. Sometimes it is helpful to do both praying and physical relaxation to get control. How do good words counter the effects of anxiety? When a person is content and balanced, then anxiety is easier to overcome. Sometimes we need others to be by our side to give us a word of comfort and perspective so that we can overcome the anxiety. Sometimes we need to get rid of the things that cause us the anxiety. However, the main answer is taking every thought captive and hiding the Word of God in your heart during these times of anxiousness. Knowing that we will not be tempted beyond what we can bear is comforting and should relieve us of much of our anxiety. Having God in control is the opposite of having anxiety in control.

Prayer: Dear Lord, in you my anxious thoughts are soothed. In my times of anxiety, I give you control of my fears, my thoughts. Lighten my heart with your Word, for it is in your Word that I am healed and my anxious thoughts are taken away. Amen.

Personal Reflections: List some things that cause you anxiety. Find passages from the Bible that help you with these causes. Make a plan to get rid of those things that you can get rid of in your life.

_____

_____

_____

_____

_____

_____

_____

_____

_____

_____

_____

_____

_____

_____

_____

_____

_____

_____

_____

Plans of the heart. (Prov. 16:1-3)

"The plans of the heart belong to man, but the answer of the tongue is from the Lord. .. Commit your works to the Lord, and your plans will be established."

As I write this section, I am waiting for a dream job to come through. It would be a wonderful opportunity to expand the kingdom through evangelism and missions. It would also take care of our financial needs that have been so wanting, being a missionary. The second verse says that the Lord looks at our motives to see if they are selfish, or in line with God's plan. I hope that my whole life is given to God and His plans. I do not know if I will get this new ministry I still will continue to work for the Lord in whatever and where ever He will lead me. What are your plans for your life? Maybe you should ask, "What does God want for my life? Have you ever thought about it this way? Not all of us will be ministers, missionaries, or leaders, but all can include God in their plans for life. You must ask, was God in my decision for my vocation or occupation? Is God in your plans today? I am afraid that most people choose their way of life without including God. Maybe God will be included when the plan you have made goes wrong. We tend to ask for help when we have come to our wits end, instead of including Him from the beginning. Some may be afraid to include God because He may call them into some ministry or work for Him. I can attest that is not a bad choice, rather it is a much better great choice. Can God be in your plans if you're not in fulltime ministry? Of course, God needs disciples in every walk of life. Your plans include your relationships, your marriage, and every aspect of your life. Is God in every plan you make? Remember: He knows your heart and motives; therefore, let Him be a part at every point so that you will always be within His will and eventually be successful in Him. How do you include Him in your plans? You must pray for his wisdom and guidance. You must also know His will for your life.

Prayer: Lord, help my plans to be your plans. Forgive me when I have gone my way and not included you in what I do, or the plans I have made. Lord, I want to be successful in your eyes within your plans. Teach me your way. I pray this in your precious name. Amen.

Personal Reflections: Make two list. First, express where God has been in some of your plans. Second, where has He not been. What was the result of each?

_____

_____

_____

_____

_____

_____

_____

_____

_____

_____

_____

_____

_____

_____

_____

_____

_____

_____

_____

_____

_____

Prudent Heart (discerning) (Proverbs 18:15)

The mind (heart) of the prudent acquires Knowledge."

The two key words are mind or heart, and prudent. Heart mind and Kidneys are sometimes interchanged in the Old Testament. The heart is the center of the human existence. The person that develops a prudent heart acquires or seeks out knowledge. This acquired knowledge can be used in everyday life to make a better decision in the world. The book of Proverbs is a guide to practical and Godly living. If a person is prudent, shrewd, or discerning then he will search out the knowledge that is useful. What kind of knowledge should you search for to be prudent? Not just any knowledge. The word of God often contrasts good and bad knowledge, in some cases even useless. But in this context, we can assume that the knowledge is based in truth and God. Knowledge is good if it leads to growth or beneficial outcome for everyone involved. I am afraid that in this day that we all have a possibility of information overload, information that leads to nowhere in the end, or at least to a mundane life. What is the opposite meaning of this verse? It is foolishness that lies in ignorance. Ignorance is the root of a lot of evil and mishaps in life. Knowledge is the underpinning of hope and future progression, but ignorance brings harm because what you do not know will usually lead to decisions that will be negative circumstances in your life. Acquiring knowledge that leads to health, happiness, and godliness is a goal that each of us should work toward. To acquire knowledge you must work at it. Good knowledge does not come by osmosis; you must work at finding it, or at least learn what it looks like when it falls into your hands. Be open to new information, and you will grow in knowledge. More important is to be open to God's information and you will grow eternal benefits.

Prayers: Lord, help me to acquire the right knowledge. The right knowledge that leads to You is what I need to live. Help me not to be ignorant of your love and blessings, but rather be ignorant of the ways of the world. I pray this in your precious name. amen.

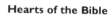

Personal Reflections: It is easy to lists what you do know, but better to list things you don't know but need to know, and write what you have to do to acquire God's knowledge found in His word.

_____

_____

_____

_____

_____

_____

_____

_____

_____

_____

_____

_____

_____

_____

_____

_____

_____

_____

_____

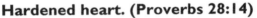

Hardened heart. (Proverbs 28:14)
"How blessed is the man who always fears, But he who hardens his heart will fall into calamity."

How many calamities did Pharaoh have? Have you wondered why God continued to harden Pharaoh's heart? God knew that Pharaoh hardened his own heart due to sin, and God used that to His purpose. Pharaoh had little, or no, fear of Moses God because he saw himself as god. In other words, he was delusional about his grandeur. Therefore, his heart was hardened more than most, and his calamity was more than most of history. How many calamities have you had in your life? Was any of it because of your hardness of heart? Was it because you do not fear God for who He is? Or, in your eyes you're o.k. And there is no fear or awe in your life towards God? There is no way a person who is in awe of God can harden his heart. You notice the person in this passage decides to harden his heart. It is also the man who chooses to fear always. Both are in the hands of each of us, and we have the free will to choose either way and, therefore, are responsible for the calamity in our lives. Not all calamities are a result of our choices, like many of the Egyptians I would imagine. But we can be assured that when we do fail to fear God and decide to harden our heart we will assuredly fall into the calamity of our own doing. What are the results of godly fear? It will be a heart that does not spurn God's ways. A soft heart leads to openness to God and His will. What are the blessings that we are promised? The opposite of calamity is harmony and fruitfulness of life. Calamity stops the progression of life and its blessings. Therefore become open to God and do not harden your heart then you will not create disaster for yourself and others around you. What are those blessings of being in fear or awe of God? Let us name a few. Companionship, security, eternal reward, respect of who He is. I can go on, but simply it is all out worship that results when we are in awe of God our Creator.

Prayer: Lord, please help me to soften my heart and not harden it. Help me to fear you in your holiness. Help me to be in awe of your greatness. Please protect me from mine and others calamity so I might serve you always.

Personal Reflections: List some of the calamities that have happened in your life. You might see where it was a result from the hardness of your heart. Think of ways you need to soften your heart.

_____

_____

_____

_____

_____

_____

_____

_____

_____

_____

_____

_____

_____

_____

_____

_____

_____

_____

Self-righteous heart (Proverbs 28:26)

"He who trusts in his own heart is a fool, but he who walks wisely will be delivered."

Why is he a fool who trust in his own heart? We have to consider the source. Our heart is blanketed with holes of inconsistency, sin, and sometimes plain old stupidity. So, why should we trust in it? Some might say, "Some have common sense, and others do not." Where did that common sense come from? If it is based in truth, then God is the source. It is important to realize even common sense can be misguided if it is based in man's wisdom, which in many cases can masquerade as common sense. If the wisdom is common to man, then it may make no sense at all and lead us to follow the folly of man. Sometimes common sense to man is not common, or sensible at all according to God's truth. What does it mean to walk wisely? To realize that we do not know it all, and that we need to trust in the Lord. This trust is the beginning of wisdom and the negation of foolishness. The wise will walk in the counsel and Word of God, not in our wisdom. What happens if we do not? We must realize that our unwise walking will lead us into trouble and self-deceit. We will stumble and fall, and in some cases not get up, or worse fall to our spiritual death. It will lead to self-deceit when we think that man's wisdom or common sense is a valid way of walking. What do we need to be delivered from? We need to be delivered from our self, from Satan, and from death. That is death in this life, and the life to come. God wants us to walk with Him each day and not after our or others foolish ways. The problem is that many today do not believe in absolutes, but rather in their foolish relative ways. When we walk in God's wisdom we will have a better life as well as in the life to come.

Prayer: Lord, please deliver me from my path that I make each day. Number my steps that I may not stumble. Show me my foolishness and make in me a heart that trusts in You, so that I may walk in a manner that is pleasing to you. I do not want to trust in my own heart. I pray this in your precious name. Amen.

Personal Reflections: List some ways you have walked foolishly in the past week. Conversely, list some ways you walked wisely. What were the results in both?

_____

_____

_____

_____

_____

_____

_____

_____

_____

_____

_____

_____

_____

_____

_____

_____

_____

_____

_____

Deceived Heart (Isaiah 44:20)
"He feeds on ashes; a deceived heart has turned him aside. And he cannot deliver himself."

What is so dangerous about a deceived heart? The problem in being deceived is that you think you are right when you are dead wrong. When a person thinks he is right, then it is foolishness to tell him he is wrong because he will not believe you and will become defensive or argumentative. People like this think they are right; then you must be wrong. When these people are in this state of delusion, they cannot help themselves get out of the "circular reasoning." If they are right, then how can the opposition be right and they too at the same time? Therefore, they must be right and, therefore, stay within their belief system. For that person to be helped, several things must happen. The opposing person must try to help the other person to see the truth. That will take this person knowing the truth and how to explain both why it is true, and why the deceived person's way is inconsistent with reality. Second, the helper must realize that every one of us has our own worldview, and this is the place each one starts in their reasoning of their position. Third, the deceived person must genuinely want to know the truth. That is; he must believe in absolutes. If people like this do not, then it is hopeless to change or convince them otherwise. This is where prayer for the power and influence of the Spirit must be present throughout the process. How can they be turned from ignorance to the truth? They must turn from being deceived. How do they get deceived about their beliefs? One way is that they do not think for themselves; they allow others to make their minds up. When they are deceived, they must have help to get out of their deluded state. Jesus is the only hope to help a person out of their state and be delivered by the power of the Holy Spirit. Last, each person must come to realize he cannot deliver himself. This is hard, but not impossible with the Lord and a friend to show them.

Prayer: Lord, I ask for your enlightenment of your truth that I might recognize the deception that myself and others are under. Give me the wisdom to not be deceived and to help others who are. In Jesus name, Amen

Personal Reflections: Personal Reflections: Think about something you might have been deceived about. Now think of how you came out of it.

_____

_____

_____

_____

_____

_____

_____

_____

_____

_____

_____

_____

_____

_____

_____

_____

_____

_____

_____

_____

_____

Cleansed Heart (Proverbs 20: 9)
" Who can say, I have cleansed my heart, I am pure from my sin"?

Can you say yes to this proverb? I cannot. No one can say this but Jesus himself. Jesus never had to cleanse His heart; it was clean from the start. Can we clean our heart? Again, no we cannot; we do not have the ability on our own to cleanse our heart. Would you clean something with a dirty rag? Of course not, you would contaminate even more what you're trying to clean. It's just like doing the wrong over and over and thinking at some point the right desired result will finally happen. Same is the case when we try to clean our self, by our means. Our righteousness is as filthy rags, so we need something from outside ourselves to clean us. Only in Jesus can that be so. Only in Jesus can we have the means and power to have a cleansed heart and be pure from sin. We must participate in this process. We must renew our minds, and we must set our hearts and minds on being pure. It is our choice to make it happen, but it is not in our power to make it happen. When we choose to be cleansed, we must make up our minds to make the changes from an unclean heart or actions to a clean one. That is, when our temptation is to be impure, we now make the clean choice to do what is right. When we make this choice, we must call on the power of God to help us carry it through. The key is that we must be cleansed by the power of the Spirit through being in a right relationship with Jesus as our lord through being His disciple. When this happens, He cleanses us from our sin and purifies our hearts. Now, I can say I am cleansed in my heart and pure from my sin because of my Lord Jesus. It is not that we are sinless, but we must strive to sin less each day, that is the process of becoming cleansed and growing spiritually.

Prayer: Lord, I come to you not knowing fully what it means to have a cleansed heart, but that is what I want from day to day. I know when I am cleansed in heart, I am cleansed from my sin. Lord thanks for your cleansing, and for forgiving me of my sin. Your purity is my hope for the same. In your name, Amen.

Personal Reflections: Think of some things that show both your pure and not so pure heart. What can you do to get rid of one, and strengthen the other?

_____

_____

_____

_____

_____

_____

_____

_____

_____

_____

_____

_____

_____

_____

_____

_____

_____

_____

_____

_____

Closed Heart (I John 3:17)

"But whoever has the world's goods, and beholds his brother in need and closes his heart against him, how does the love of God abide in him?"

This is a riveting verse for those who are rich. What does it mean to be rich, or what does it mean for a person to have the world's goods? There is no excuse for a person who is rich, not to give to those who are in need. There are many stories of those who are milked because they are rich. Are the wealthy always obligated to take care of the poor? I guess if they can, they should, but Jesus said the poor are always with us. The key in this verse is "brother" We are not totally responsible for every person in the world, but we are for those who are in the brotherhood. If we see a brother in the community in need then we need to help him. If we have two coats, and are brother has none then should we not give them one? This is not welfare all the time, but I know of times when I have been in need and a brother has come along and helped. One winter when I could not afford the gas bill, and the body came through with help. This Christmas we helped a family up the road have a Christmas by giving their children some presents. There is a line between helping people till they get on their feet and continually giving to a person that is taking advantage. In my mission travels, I have opportunity actually to give some water to a person in need or buy a person some food. The key is not to close our hearts to people in need that we meet. We should not become suckers to those scammers, but if we let the Lord lead and give from the heart then God will bless us and others. Being a disciple is about having a compassionate heart, not a stingy, closed heart. I have unknowingly given to scammers from a good heart, and God will deal with them. But, how can we know whether the one we give to will either be an angel or a person in need who will be changed and brought to the throne of Christ by your loving act?

Prayer: Lord, give me wisdom to know when, and to whom, to give. Give me compassion, for others have given me compassion when I have been in need. Thank you, Lord, Amen

Personal Reflections: When did someone give to you when you were in need? When was the last time you gave to someone who was in need?

_____

_____

_____

_____

_____

_____

_____

_____

_____

_____

_____

_____

_____

_____

_____

_____

_____

Weighed Heart (Proverbs 21:1, 2)

"Every man's way is right in his own eyes, but the Lord weighs the hearts."

How many times do we rationalize what we think? I know in many people's lives that it is easy to convince himself that something is right when it is wrong. Many times, people go through life thinking "it is ok, everyone does it." The problem is that people have given up absolutes, and whatever feels right is right. If one does not convince himself he is right, then the guilt will come into play. If this happens too many times, then he looks for a rationalizing moment to look the other way and turn absolutes into relativism. Why do we give up absolutes in our lives? Usually, it is easier for some people to give in than to do the right thing. Most do not want the absolute/truth telling them how they should act or think. Most have been convinced that things are relative these days without the need for many absolutes. Furthermore, many do not know what absolutes are or have never been taught they exist or are important in this day and age. This is sad, many even in the Church have fewer absolutes than before. Even when we convince ourselves we are right, God truly knows our hearts, even when we do not know our own. Even when we think we are right, and we are dead wrong. What will make a difference? Only when we know the Word will we know what absolute/truth is. When we allow the Spirit to guide us we will move closer to absolute/truth, and when our hearts are weighed we will not be found wanting in His eyes. Let us strive to live by God's absolutes and not the ways of man. Frank Sinatra sang, "I did it my way" and so many people today take this as their theme song. If Jesus is the way, the truth, and the life, then we cannot have it both ways. Either there are absolutes or not. Either He is right, or man is right. How do you want the results of Jesus weighing of your heart?

Prayer: Lord, you know us when we don't even know ourselves. Please reveal to me what are my inner thoughts, and help me be honest with myself, which is the hardest thing to do sometimes dear Lord. Help me get myself out of the way and let you be my guide.

Personal Reflections: What are some things in your life that you thought were right, but you found were wrong? What struggles do you have that you need to give over to the Lord? Be honest with yourself and God.

_____

_____

_____

_____

_____

_____

_____

_____

_____

_____

_____

_____

_____

_____

_____

_____

_____

Kind Heart (I Peter 3:8)

"To sum up let all be harmonious, sympathetic, brotherly, kindhearted, and humble in spirit."

What is Peter trying to say here? He is continuing to help us learn how to treat and live with each other. Peter is talking to both husbands and wives, who need to treat each other with a kind heart. What does this mean? Do you give respect when you talk with your spouse, treating each with gentle actions? Or do you act disrespectfully in how you say things or respond? These directions give practical ways of dealing and interacting with your spouse or any other person you come to deal with in life. I guess a rude person has a hard time being kind-hearted towards others. Is this a personality flaw or just being inconsiderate? I have heard that in many cases where men grow up to mistreat people, and even display bodily harm, that as a child they were mean or destructive to animals. What I am saying here is that a kind heart is developed in two ways. First, it is illustrated to the youth by their parents and caregivers. Secondly, it comes from having God make a difference in their life. I believe a non-kind-hearted person is not a Spirit-filled or led person. If you have a problem with being kindhearted, then look at your life with Christ and His Spirit. Non-believers can be kindhearted because of their upbringing. And Christians at times can lack in their kindheartedness towards others. Being kindhearted is both a learned trait and a Spiritual one. To be kindhearted, we must renew our minds and be willing to change our ways so that we show kindness to others. The best way is to allow the Holy Spirit to give us that power to be kindhearted to everyone, even when we do not feel like it. The non-believer kindhearted will not do it when they do not feel like it. Go and show some random acts of kindness from your heart today and see what comes back to you. How do you act when it is hard to be kind? Remember Jesus is always kind and as his disciple we too must strive to be like Him.

Prayer: Help me be kindhearted to my spouse, my family, and my fellow man. Let everyone see my kind heart. In Jesus Name, Amen.

Personal Reflections: In the past couple of days have you either been kind-hearted or lacking in this area? Note either or both, and how you can be better in this area.

_____

_____

_____

_____

_____

_____

_____

_____

_____

_____

_____

_____

_____

_____

_____

_____

_____

_____

—

Hidden Heart (I Peter 3:4)

"But let it be the hidden person of the heart with the imperishable quality of a gentle and quiet spirit which is precious in the sight of God."

Peter is specifically talking with women in this context, but this is in no way rare in men today. It is true that some women spend a lot of time on fixing themselves up on the outside. Men may wash, shave their face and comb their hair, but that is usually the extent of grooming. Most women though add about ten different steps to the process of getting ready to tackle the day. This <u>can</u> be a source of pride for both men and women. Of course, the outside is the first we see of a person and in some cases, like job interviews, a deal breaking aspect. In some cases, though it does not take long for what is inside to overshadow the outside charade. Peter is stressing that what we consider precious, or important on the outside, is nothing to God who looks on the inside for pure beauty. Who is the true person, the true hidden heart in you? Are you shallow in your thoughts, your relationships, and in your quality of life and commitment? Or do you have His quiet, humble Spirit, and does not need outside props to make you feel good when inside you are dying and unfulfilled? If you truly have the light and love of God then what is felt by you, and seen by others, is a gentle and beautiful spirit guided by the love and Spirit of God. Put some makeup on but not at the expense and time to spend on your inner beauty. Think about it. Do you spend more time each day on your face and hair than you have on devotions with God? God does not want a shallow relationship with His children. Sadly, in most cases we do not know our hidden person. Open up to God and ask Him to reveal to you your true self and how to become gentle like Jesus. Each of us, man or woman must strive to develop the inner qualities that become precious in the sight of God.

Prayer: Let Your gentleness and humbleness be evident in my life. Let me be your beloved child. Your beauty in me is what I need. In Jesus Name, amen.

Personal Reflections: How much time do you spend on both your devotions and outer appearance?. If it is the latter, think of ways to take a little more from the outer and spend more time with God.

_____

_____

_____

_____

_____

_____

_____

_____

_____

_____

_____

_____

_____

_____

_____

_____

_____

Evil Heart (Genesis 8:21)

"And the Lord smelled the soothing aroma and the Lord said to Himself, I will never again curse the ground on account of man, for the intent of man's heart is evil from his youth and I will never again destroy every living thing as I have done."

Why will God not destroy the world again like that? I think when God smelled Noah's offering of the animal sacrifice, He let us know that it was not the earth, nor the animals that were the problem, but the man from his youth. What is this saying? First, that children are blank slates to be written on. They can be brought up in the ways of the Lord, and when they are older will not depart from them. But if we do not capture our youth before they become teenagers or later adolescence, then we have a good chance of having wayward youth and adults. That which is bred in young people in their earlier years will affect the condition and consciousness of their heart. The Biblical saying that "to spare the rod spoils the child," is important in our training our youth. Having no discipline will result in the possibility of evil intent and thoughts in their minds and hearts. There are exceptions in both scenarios, but the basic truth is there. As you read this where are you in the equation? First, are you a parent that was absent in bringing up your child with God-fearing principles? Second, are you one who was not disciplined in your youth and have found evil intent, and continue to struggle now? Third, are you in your developing years and find that you have unhealthy thoughts and actions? Then I say to all three, there is hope if you want to make that change and come under the love and discipline of your loving Father and Lord Jesus Christ. What is the intent of your heart? Only when you present your life as a sweet aroma will God be pleased.

Prayer: Lord, help all those who deal with children to remember to write upon them the Word of God and the love you can show them. I pray for those who have been allowed to grow with the evil intent that you provide an opportunity and a contrite heart that they may turn to know your love and way. In the Lord, Amen

Personal Reflections: Have you seen any signs of evil in you or your children's hearts? Don't worry if you are training them in the ways of the Lord.

_____

_____

_____

_____

_____

_____

_____

_____

_____

_____

_____

_____

_____

_____

_____

_____

_____

_____

_____

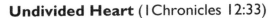

Undivided Heart (I Chronicles 12:33)

"Of Zebulon there were 50,000 who went out in the army, who could draw up in battle formation with all kinds of weapons of war and helped David with an undivided heart."

What is the worst that could happen to a leader of an army? What could make him want to give up? What could make him so mad he could shoot someone? A soldier that is undependable and divided in his loyalty. Another word for this behavior is "traitor." You cannot trust a person that is divided in heart and loyalty. These men of Zebulon were men with undivided hearts in their dedication to David and his battle. They had all the weapons they needed, but their main contribution was their heart, their will to be dedicated and one in purpose and strength. What God wants from each of us is that we have an undivided heart in our devotion to His army. What is it like to have an undivided heart? You will be focused on your allegiance to God and not your agenda. You will no longer be lukewarm, but rather on fire in your devotion and growth. You will not let the worldly things control factors in your life. The synonym to undivided is "loyalty." The more you follow Christ as His disciple, the more the struggle between your past and His presence in your life will be lessened. You will be able to overcome temptations and you will not be overcome to the point of having to make a choice between your old life, tempting friends and the world, but rather be totally committed and undivided in your heart. Are you undivided in your faith and doubts toward God? If so, you will be stable and sure of your faith and Jesus will count you with His army. Jesus said you cannot serve two masters. That is, you cannot serve yourself and God at the same time. Choose this day who you will serve. If you do choose God, you too will be victorious in your life and welcomed into God's army. And He will say one day, "Come in my faithful servant."

Prayer: Lord, when you look at my heart I pray that you see an undivided heart towards You and Your Word, having an undivided devotion to follow and not shrink back. Help me to be steadfast and focused on you. I pray in your precious name. Amen.

Personal Reflections: Think of anything that may divide your heart. List them and pray for how to deal with those issues.

_____

_____

_____

_____

_____

_____

_____

_____

_____

_____

_____

_____

_____

_____

_____

_____

_____

_____

_____

_____

_____

Heart that spurns correction (Proverbs 5:12)

"And you say how I have hated instruction and my heart spurned reproof."

We have two issues in this little passage, but what is far from simplistic. If a person fails in these two areas in life, they will most likely find that they are going to have a long miserable existence. What is a person called who does not want to listen to instruction? Some would say stubborn, foolish, or just plain stupid. Some might even call him rebellious and ignorant. What is the result of hating instruction? When you hate instruction you might say, you hate yourself because you are sabotaging your future. Without instruction, there is no wisdom or hope for a future, nor desire to know who God is and how He wants to know you. The second issue is rejecting correction. But what are the consequences of having a heart that refuses correction. We have already talked some about the results of sparing the rod and spoiling the child. When something spoils, it is usually no good and of no use to anyone. Correction is going the wrong way and being guided in a new direction. If we are not willing to be under correction, then we are not under the authority of God. My heart, my inner being does not want to hear what may be the best for me to hear. When a person comes to the knowledge of Christ what he must hear is reproof. That is; you are a sinner and you need to turn from your evil ways. A person with a contrite heart will receive reproof and the person who does not will spurn this reproof and be lost forever. To receive reproof one must have a heart of repentance, and humbleness to accept the correction that is given. This applies to both a new believer and the seasoned saint. There is little hope for change when the heart turns away from correction because we are all in a state of rebellion and must relinquish our pride and accept the correction that is given, or we cannot change. Do you want change? Then listen to your Lord.

Prayer: Lord, help me when I need to follow your instruction and your correction, even when it may hurt. Lord your correction is my hope for a new life in you. In Jesus' Name, Amen

Personal Reflections: Do you have a problem with being corrected? How can you let God help? What lessons have you learned from both rejecting and accepting correction.

Heart that turns away (Deuteronomy 29:18)

"Lest there shall be among you a man or woman, or family or tribe whose <u>heart turns away</u> today from the Lord our God, to go and serve the gods of those nations, lest there shall be among you a root bearing poisonous fruit and wormwood."

What a sad set of circumstances when a person turns away from the Lord. Can a believer's heart turn away from God? Some say it is impossible, but in the New Testament it is obvious that a man of faith can become, by his choice, a man without faith. Each person choses to follow or believe in Jesus and we can choose to not follow. I Timothy 4:1 says "in later times some will fall away from the faith." How can they fall from faith if they never had faith? Being in the faith means they were in a state of salvation at that point. "Fall from faith" means they lose their salvation. To say they never were believers is calling the Word and the Spirit liars. The moment a person begins to turn from God then he must turn back, or he will continue to go deeper in sin to the point they turn away for good if they do not repent. They will then again serve another god. Maybe the one they were following before they followed God, or a new god that has enticed them to fall away. The moment a person begins to go away from God a seed of discontent and evil begins to take root, until it bears poisonous fruit that turns both the believer sour, and God sick with them and their walk. Each one of us must "Choose this day whom you will serve," and each day after that. Not in your might or strength, but in the name of Jesus as your Lord and the power of the Word and Spirit as your guide. The temptation of the eyes is the first step of turning away to other gods, and other gods will poison the heart away from their first love. If it is allowed to progress it will affect the whole body. Protect your heart from being poisoned by continuing in faith with God. Be of good cheer and not fear if your trying to walk with God in your daily life. God will protect and guide those who follow.

Prayer: Lord, protect my heart that it will not turn away from you. Take any bitter root in me and burn it. Through your Spirit give me the power to follow you all my life. In Jesus name, amen.

Personal Reflections: Think very deeply for this is crucial idea that if we deny the possibility of falling then we may fall, and if we neglect it we will fall. Think of any thoughts or doubts in your faith, then give them to God.

_____

_____

_____

_____

_____

_____

_____

_____

_____

_____

_____

_____

_____

_____

_____

_____

_____

_____

Sincere Heart (Hebrews 10:21, 22)

"let us draw near with a <u>sincere heart</u> in full assurance of faith having our hearts sprinkled clean from an evil conscience and our bodies washed with pure water."

The focus in this passage is "we now have a great High Priest" in Jesus. Therefore, we can come before or draw near to God because Jesus fulfilled the penalty of sin and since the veil is now split, we have access to God. It is our choice whether to draw near to God. When we do we need to do it with a sincere heart. From the beginning God wanted us to be true and sincere with our hearts, emotions, mind, and will toward Him. Jesus had the most problems with people who called themselves God-followers and did it with a hypocritical heart or lifestyle. God sees our hearts and knows when we are true believers. He will reward those who earnestly seek Him with a sincere heart. The next aspect in this passage is that a sincere heart is established in faith. Without faith, we cannot please God, or approach His throne now or in the future. We have full assurance because our assurance is in Jesus and not in ourselves. This full assurance comes when we are washed in pure water of the Word and Baptism thus cleansing our conscience, through contact with both. A person has an evil conscience when he is not sincere in heart. Having a sincere heart is at the center of this passage. If we want to draw near, we must sincerely want to be a follower and lover of God. Without sincerity, one cannot have a true saving faith. Without a sincere heart you cannot be purified from your sin. Sincerity is mandatory for your conscience to be free from evil. For the opposite of sincerity is a lie, the root of an evil heart. Where is your sincerity level? When was the last time you drew near to God? It is when we humbly draw near that He can help us with that sincere heart we so need.

Prayer: Lord, you see my heart better than I or anyone else. I want to be sincere and full of faith through your cleansing of me in pure water. Help me to stay pure and sincere as I draw near in all I say and do. I pray this in your precious name. Amen.

Personal Reflections: Think about your drawing near, your conscience, your assurance in Him, and your contact with pure water. Which of them do you lack? What can you do to make each aspect in line with the will of God?

_____

_____

_____

_____

_____

_____

_____

_____

_____

_____

_____

_____

_____

_____

_____

_____

_____

Slow of heart (Luke 24:25)

"And He said to them, O foolish men and slow of heart to believe in all that the prophets have spoken."

Have you ever been accused of being a slowpoke? I have been called one and I have also called others the same. Being a slowpoke is usually a derogatory term for those who can't keep up. Is being a slowpoke by choice? I think you can look at it in two ways. First, you may be the slowest in the pack. That is, no matter how hard you try, you will fall behind because others are faster than you. Second, you may choose to be a slowpoke. That is, you decide not to try, or you just like going slow and not being in a hurry. In these situations you choose to be slow and there is really no excuse. Some in Jesus' day chose to be slow in hearing or believing the message of the Messiah foretold by the prophets. Jesus did not reveal to them who he was so that he could get them to be honest in what they believed about all that had just happened. They failed the test. Is your heart slow to hear and believe God's son Jesus? If so, then you're a fool as well. Jesus is talking to those who knew what the prophets had predicted, God's own people were looking, but not truly seeing the truth that was in front of them. From time to time I have worshiped with a local Messianic congregation and I have noticed their whole problem is as it was 2,000 years ago. To convince the Jews that Jesus is the one the prophets have told us about, and that He has come, and is coming back again. Are they going to be ready? Are you going to be ready, or will you be slow of heart in believing that Jesus the Messiah was and is still real today? You must choose not to be foolish of heart. Before we chastise these men, we must put ourselves in their shoes. Do you truly believe all that you have heard and seen about Jesus? Are you slow to believe in his grace and beautiful promises of life and joy? Come closer today and rejoice.

Prayer: Lord, please help my slow heart to believe all that you have said about yourself and your plan of life. Lord, forgive me when I am foolish and do not believe all that you have done for us. Help me to trust in your Word and the prophets. Amen.

Personal Reflections: What things have you been slow of heart about? Write down two or three things that you have a hard time believing. Repent of any foolishness in your life.

_____

_____

_____

_____

_____

_____

_____

_____

_____

_____

_____

_____

_____

_____

_____

_____

Doing good heart (Galatians 6:9)

"Let us not lose heart in doing good, for in due time we will reap if we do not grow weary. "

I had a hard time in determining, whether this statement is about doing good or losing heart. I guess you can't have a ying without a yang. First, there must be the opposite of this proposition. It assumes that one can lose heart in doing good. This means that a person may do a lot of good things and get no rewards at first. The person may help people and get no thanks, or he may do something great for someone, and someone else gets the credit. The key here is what is the motive for doing good? If the motive for doing good is to get recognition then when you do not get that recognition you will grow weary in continuing to do good things. Eventually, the doing good will cease. If the motive is altruistic, and for the love of God and people, then it would not be disconcerting to not get the recognition when the act is done. The Bible indicates if the motive is to be recognized, then you will receive your reward in the recognition. If it is a pure motive, then it is important not to grow weary. If it is the second motive, then the reward is better delayed. For the "in Due time" may be at the discretion of God who does the rewarding. You may receive some recognition in the moment, and that is encouraging. If it is never realized on this earth God will for sure give you a better reward on His time table. Nothing is better than to hear someone you helped say, "what you have done has changed my life, or saved me." At this point it is the difference in which motive drives you. If you immediately give all credit to God in your words and heart, then God is glorified. If you take the praise personally then you are glorified and you have your reward. But the encouragement is not to lose heart, for those who are the recipients of your goodness are blessed, and that is rewarding. Never forget that what you do will make a difference, so rejoice.

Prayer: Lord, help me first to do good in any way I can. Help my motives to be pure so that I will not lose heart or seek recognition. Let my doing good be good for others. I pray in your name. Amen.

Personal Reflections: Remember three good things you have done this past month. Did you get any recognition for them? How did you feel in each case?

_____

_____

_____

_____

_____

_____

_____

_____

_____

_____

_____

_____

_____

_____

_____

_____

_____

_____

_____

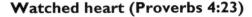

Watched heart (Proverbs 4:23)

"Watch over your heart with all diligence for from it flows the springs of life."

Most believers fail when they do not watch and pray. What are we to watch over? What do we let into our hearts or minds? What do we look at? What do we do on weekends, or when the curtain is closed? What do we do on the web? What do we think about? These are questions we must ask ourselves each day because at any given moment we can be overcome by the world. God does not care about what we say as much as what we think for He knows that what we say comes from what we think. A spring is what naturally brings fresh water to other sources of water, but it can be contaminated to where it is no longer of use. We must be diligent to see that it is kept pure from contamination from the world. Let us not convince our self that we are okay when we truly are not. If we think of bad things, and do bad things, then we are bad, if we make it a lifestyle. We are all at times going to do bad things and think bad things, it is our human nature. However, the goal of discipleship is that we replace our human nature with God's Spirit and His nature. The more we replace our nature with His, then the less we will act on our human nature. It is our duty to be diligent to watch our heart and the way we think. We have no excuse if we fail. To make the changes each person must allow the Spirit to flow from his heart. We cannot do it on our own, but we must partner with the Spirit to make it happen. One without the other will end in polluted springs of life. This is a spiritual experience with power that comes only from God. The amazing thing is that the blessings that come with our diligence will pay off with wonderful experiences with God. We must be diligent to protect our heart in God. Jesus told us that springs of living water will flow if we follow Him. Our heart is where Christ is dwelling, resulting in springs of living water.

Prayer: Father, help me to be diligent to watch over my heart. Help me not to pollute my springs with a heart that is not walking in your light. In Jesus' name, amen.

Personal Reflections: List the things you have to watch in your mind and heart. Pray then for the Spirit to give you the power to watch over your heart.

_____

_____

_____

_____

_____

_____

_____

_____

_____

_____

_____

_____

_____

_____

_____

_____

_____

Misdirected Heart (Numbers 15:39)

"And it shall be a tassel for you to look at and remember all the commandments of the Lord so as to do them and not follow after your own heart, and your own eyes after which you played the harlot."

How does anyone know what is right or wrong? An earlier devotion talked about the importance of being in the Word and to know what is absolute, and what is relative. When did the Israelites get into trouble? When they looked away from God's commands and sought other gods and ways of life. It is very easy to forget when we do not have a visual reminder in front of us. It is easy to go back to the road of least resistance. This is why God wanted His people to be reminded of His commands. I just returned from my first trip to Israel. While there I bought my wife a prayer shawl and blessed it at the western wall. On the shawl are tassels like God called His people to use to remember His commandments, even till this day. Why do we follow only our own heart? It is because we do not know His heart. We many times pretend to be with Him at church or in devotions, but do we keep His commandments in front of mind and heart? Most of us do not. When this happens, it is easy to go astray and play the harlot with the god of ourselves, the god of our own eyes, and other gods may follow. Do not be selfish with your own heart; give it wholly to the Lord. We do not know God's heart as we should. Until our heart is like His heart we will never truly have the relationship with Him that we were meant to have. To have this relationship we must make our heart, will, and wishes His wishes. Not that we give up all we desire, but in Him we will learn to desire what is in His heart, and it will be better than ours. If his word is in your heart you will be protected from a wandering heart. God is good. His principles are for the health of our heart.

Prayer: Lord, keep your tassels in front of our eyes that we may never forget your loving commands and will for our lives. Lord, help me to not follow after my own ways or eyes, but after yours alone. In your precious name, amen.

Personal Reflections: Take a look at some of the commands we see in the Old and New Testament to see where we stand. Pick a few and try to follow them this week.

_____

_____

_____

_____

_____

_____

_____

_____

_____

_____

_____

_____

_____

_____

_____

_____

_____

_____

_____

Melodious Heart (Ephesians 5:19)

"Speaking to one another in psalms and hymns and spiritual songs, singing and making melody with your heart to the Lord."

What was the last song you sang? Was it a song on the radio, mp3, or the person next to you humming in the elevator? I usually continue to sing the last song I heard; do you too? It is funny and sometimes embarrassing singing songs you just heard. You can make melody in your heart to something that is not to uplifting or edifying. Whatever comes out of your mouth still comes from the heart. It is important to be careful what you listen to. Songs have made a difference in shaping many peoples' lives. How many spiritual songs have moved us to be better? How many secular songs have led us away? It is important to realize that songs are powerful. Notice in the passage above. The important thing is not only making melody with your heart. It is what comes before; it is the object of what you make melody with. If you are "speaking to one another in psalms, hymns and spiritual songs." then when you sing one of these types of songs then the melody in heart will be pleasing to the Lord. When you sing these types of songs you're singing either scripture or spiritual songs. In verse 20 it says to always give thanks. If we have true joy and sing from the heart and have this attitude in us, we will be able to give thanks for He is the one who should put that melody in our heart. The result is that God is blessed, others who hear you are blessed, and in turn you are blessed. Notice the word "speaking" does a song, hymn or psalm speak to you? Does it make a difference when you hear the song? Does it move you? The first part of the verse is directed towards one another and the second part is to the Lord. When you sing is the focus on the Lord? God loves to hear the pure lovely melody from his disciples. Do not be afraid to sing to the Lord and to each other. When you do from the heart you are blessed, others are blessed, and God is blessed. Sing, Sing, Sing.

Prayer: I rejoice in you Lord. I sing praises to you Lord from deep in my heart. I pray my melody will be in tune with you and bless you. In Jesus, Amen

Personal Reflections: list all the songs you listen to. Are they black, or would you sing them in the presence of the Lord. If black then repent and change what you listen to because they will form your heart either way. Think of your favorite songs and sing it.

_____

_____

_____

_____

_____

_____

_____

_____

_____

_____

_____

_____

_____

_____

_____

_____

_____

_____

Uncircumcised Heart (Ezekiel 44:7)

"When you brought in foreigners uncircumcised in heart and uncircumcised in flesh to be in My sanctuary to profane it."

God is a holy God and demands holiness in His presence. This was so evident in His dealings with the children of Israel in the first testament. Strange fire was forbidden and was punished by death. In this passage the children of God were bringing in, and allowing heathen to come in to the sanctuary, men who were not in a covenant relationship with God. This was forbidden and an abomination to God. What is a person with an uncircumcised flesh? As I said they are not in a covenant relationship with God. God told Abraham to circumcise the flesh of all the men for this was a sign of the covenant with Him and His people. Even today Jews and Messianic Jews will still practice this. The messianic Believer will not do it as a means of salvation, but out of honor to God. In most cases the children of Israel obeyed the physical commands of God to the letter, but the problem was that they missed the Spiritual aspect of the Physical command. They circumcised the flesh, but not the heart. And as you see in this passage the heart was the most important. If their hearts had been circumcised then they would not have allowed these outsiders into the house of God. How do you come into the presence of God? Do you come as a foreigner in the flesh, or with a circumcised heart? If you're a foreigner then you are estranged from God and not in a covenant relationship. How do you become circumcised? You must humbly come to Him each day and develop that relationship with him. If you have made a commitment to be His disciple then you're in that relationship and He wants you to come to His throne with an open heart that is totally exposed to Him without any pretentions. That is what is meant by being circumcised.

Prayer: Oh Lord, please search my heart and see that it is circumcised, that it is unhindered in its devotion to you. And Lord as I approach your holy throne, I pray I am in a holy covenant with you. In Jesus' name I pray, Amen.

Personal Reflections: Write down some things that keep your heart from being totally open. What can you do to make your covenant relationship with Him stronger?

_____

_____

_____

_____

_____

_____

_____

_____

_____

_____

_____

_____

_____

_____

_____

_____

_____

_____

Adulterous Heart (Matthew 5:28)

"But I say to you that everyone who looks on a woman to lust for her has committed adultery with her already in his heart."

I really do not like this verse. I really have a hard time in understanding fully when one crosses the line and goes from thought to sin. There are key words in this verse that give us a clue to its meaning. There are many ways to look at a woman or man, because women as well commit this sin of lusting after men in their heart. You can look at another person with admiration, with pity, love and so forth, but to look on them with lust is a sin. You may say "oh, she is pretty," or "he is really handsome," but if it goes into fantasizing about that person to the point you see yourself doing things, or wanting to do things, or even wishing you could do things with that person, then it is a sin of lust in your heart. Sin is about intention as well as action. If your heart sins, you sin. I think there are degrees of sin in our life, and that certain sins will incur different degree of punishments. I truly believe that a mass murderer will receive a greater punishment than a person that tells a little lie. Both will go to hell if they do not follow Jesus, but that punishment will be more severe for the first one than the other. The same with lust in the heart, the person who fantasizes will be less punished than the one who goes the next step and carries it out. Now you involve two people in the sin instead of just yourself. All sin first starts in the mind, heart, or will, and then is acted out. If you can stop it at the point of thought in your heart, then you will save yourself and others much pain and sin. But if a person does not stop at the thought and continues to dwell and fantasize then it for sure is a sin. But there is help when you call on the power of the Lord and focus on Him and ask for help with your commitment to your first love. The key is to take every thought Captive in the power of the Spirit. The heart is the starting place for all good an evil. Let us strive to be children with His heart.

Prayer: Lord, help me each day to take each thought captive. When I am tempted to look on a woman with lust, give me the strength to look away and not sin. In your name, Amen

Personal Reflections: How do you take your thoughts captive? When you do not what do you do?

_____

_____

_____

_____

_____

_____

_____

_____

_____

_____

_____

_____

_____

_____

_____

_____

_____

_____

_____

_____

Meditating Heart (Psalms 19:14)

"Let the words of my mouth and the meditation of my heart be acceptable in thy sight, O Lord my rock and my redeemer."

The words of my mouth are what others hear, but only we and God can see the meditation of our heart. But what we see here is that there is an acceptable and unacceptable meditation to God, and it is our responsibility to make it acceptable to Him. An unacceptable meditation is one that focuses mainly on what you want and can benefit from, and not on what God wants you to know and understand. What is a meditating heart? To meditate you must truly take the time to think and ponder to the point that what you are meditating on is touching your soul and mind. To meditate you have to empty yourself of your extraneous thoughts of the outside world and focus on the Word and person of God. It is not a mindless act of emptiness, but again a focus on a subject of higher source, God. Furthermore, not only let the experience touch us, but also move you to allow it to make a change. It also includes just meditating to bask in His glory and Love, just to have a deeper relationship with the Godhead and hear His voice. This can be done 24/7. Sadly, most of us do not take time to meditate on His Word, and in His Spirit, I know I do not. We do all kinds of acts and rituals but do not spend the time to meditate on the Word. It is in the Word that He has spoken. Now of course we can be in conversation (Pray without ceasing) and meditate with Him and His Spirit, this is meditation too, but it cannot happen if we do not have the Word implanted in us through meditation first. I encourage you to take the time to meditate with an open and honest heart so that your meditation is acceptable to Him. Take time to be still, be quiet and listen to His Spirit and Word.

Prayer: O Lord, search me and see if my heart's meditation is pleasing to you. Lord, help me to see what you see and to make my meditations help me to grow, and that I may see you more clearly in my meditation time. I pray this in your precious name.

Personal Reflections: Find a Psalm and meditate on it so that you can bask in God, and hear His Word for you. Write down what he reveals about Himself first and you second.

_____

_____

_____

_____

_____

_____

_____

_____

_____

_____

_____

_____

_____

_____

_____

_____

_____

Waxed Heart (Psalm 22:14)

"I am poured out like water, and all my bones are out of joint. My heart is like wax. It is melted within me."

What kind of heart do we see here? How does a person get to this point in life? I think it is a positive situation that results in a person having a heart that becomes like wax. But to get to this point a person must be at a low point in their life or walk. "I am poured out" indicates that he is at his end of being in control. He is to the point that he has nothing else to give in his own strength. Then his "bones are out of joint." This is painful, this is debilitating when you're out of joint. You cannot move or function as usual, and you are forced to suffer or not do anything. Any one that is out of joint needs help to get the joints back in place, and until it takes place there is pain and dysfunction. When everything is out of place in our lives, we will be out of joint. But when we finally allow our souls to be poured out like water then the next thing will take place and that is the waxing or melting of heart. A piece of wax usually comes in a bar or cake form and it is of no worth until it is melted. A candle cannot give light until the wax melts. You cannot be a light until your heart melts. Wax also can be molded into anything. But it must be totally melted to be used and put into the mold. The question is, what kind of mold will you be poured into? It will either be the mold of the world or the Word of God. You have already been molded into the world. It is time now to be melted so that you can be put into God's mold. But this must take your will to pour out yourself and let God fill you. If you want to be the light of the world you will have to let your wax melt so that His light will shine. Remember, Jesus is the wick of our candle. It is He who makes the light, but He uses our wax to make it happen. Your heart must melt so that God can mold and work with you.

Prayer: My Lord, my mold maker, make me into your mold. Give me a heart that meditates on your Word so that I can be molded into who you want me to be. In your Name, Jesus, Amen

Personal Reflections: List some things you have to do, or get rid of to pour yourself out? See Galatians 5:16-25

Contrite Heart (Psalms 51:17)

"The sacrifices of God are a broken spirit. A broken and a contrite heart, o God, thou wilt not despise."

God is the only being who does not need to be contrite or broken. He is right where He needs to be to be true to Himself and others. In every relationship within Himself and with His creation He is in congruence with each one, but we His creation are a different story. It all started with Eve in the garden when she usurped her husbands, and God's, authority. Before both Adam and she sinned, there was no need for a broken spirit, or contrite heart, but once sin came then there began the need of mankind to be broken before God. For once sin came into the world pride followed. To become broken in spirit, you must be willing to sacrifice your own will to God and get rid of your pride before Him and man. This also takes a contrite or humble heart to do so. Both seem to go hand in hand. You cannot become contrite or humble unless you become broken before God. And you must be humble or contrite before you allow yourself to be broken. What does it mean to be contrite in heart? As I have explained it includes humbleness, brokenness, and repentance in tandem. A contrite heart is one that humbles itself to the point of repentance. If you do not repent because of a broken spirit and contrite heart, then it is doubtful there was true contrition to begin with. Look at your own relationship and self, are you broken before God? Can you humble yourself in His sight; are you contrite before God, and can you repent? If not, then go before Him and ask for His help to do so. Because this is what He requires before He listens to you or blesses you. You cannot come before God without your contrite heart and broken Spirit. And when we do, He will lift us up and bless us. Contrite heart is synonymous with being sorry for your sin with the intention of commitment to not continuing in that sin.

Prayer: My God, I want to come to you with a contrite or humble spirit that I may sacrifice my will. Look at my heart and be merciful to my broken spirit. Fill me with your Spirit that I may be in your will, O Lord, Amen.

Personal Reflections: What things keep you from having a contrite heart and broken spirit before God? List things you have been contrite for in the past, and things in the present that you need to deal with now.

_____

_____

_____

_____

_____

_____

_____

_____

_____

_____

_____

_____

_____

_____

_____

_____

_____

Deceitful Heart (Proverbs 12:20; Jer. 17:9)

"Deceit is in the heart of those who devise evil, but counselors of peace have joy."

Why does an evil person have deceit? If a person wants to do evil to someone, that person must deceive them till the act is done, or that victim may be wise to their evil ways and thwart the plans against them. Most people who act, or are evil, do so because they themselves are deceived. The devil is the great deceiver, and when he gets into the heart of a person, he deceives as he did with Eve. An evil person justifies his acts based on deceit, or else one would think why would they do this to another human being if they truly understood the implications of their actions and attitudes? Now it is easy to see how a non-believer would be deceived and use deceit in their life. But what about those who claim to be believers? First, not all who claim to be believers have truly been converted and Spirit filled. If this is the case, they are only white washed tombs. They look like believers on Sunday but the rest of the time they have not changed their evil, deceitful ways. They must rationalize their actions; that is, they deceive themselves that what they are doing is okay. In their minds the Bible is not the same today as yesterday, nor is it meant for us in our culture. Ask yourself; have you been deceitful in any of your relationships? Have you found yourself rationalizing the scripture to help you act the way you do, or believe the way you do about certain things? If so, you need to find biblical counsel that will help you see your inconsistencies for you to have joy and peace. If you think you are not touched by deceit, you are deceived. Ask God to protect your heart from the attack of the great deceiver. Rejoice that He who lives in you will keep you from deceit if you will only go to Him and ask for the protection from the evil one. When you rely on Jesus you will have joy, and when others deceive you, you know God is your confident and protector.

Prayer: Lord, search my heart and reveal to me any deceit or rationalization in my heart and life. Help me to be transparent with everyone so they can see you in me. In Jesus' name, amen.

Personal Reflections: Think of anything you may have convinced yourself is right, but does not go with the Word of God. Think of any deceit you may have had in any relationships lately.

_____

_____

_____

_____

_____

_____

_____

_____

_____

_____

_____

_____

_____

_____

_____

_____

_____

_____

_____

_____

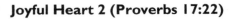

Joyful Heart 2 (Proverbs 17:22)

"A joyful heart is good medicine, but a broken spirit dries up the bones."

As in most proverbs, there is a contrast between good and the bad. We see the positive, joyful heart and the negative, broken spirit. All of us, both believers and non-believers experience both situations in our lives. A faithful growing disciple will have a better chance at having a joyful heart and being able to overcome a broken spirit. A joyful heart sees life with hope and joy. As followers and joint heirs with Christ, each of us should have joy in our hearts about life. If we do, we will have a healthy outlook, which leads to a healthy life both physically and mentally. A proven medical fact is that a person that has a healthy joyful attitude will have fewer problems in general. There are exceptions such as heredity and outside forces that may alter the outcome, but for the most part, a joyful attitude enhances health. It is reported that 75% of people's health problems stem from poor mental health. Many people have broken spirits because they have had low self-esteem. They have been broken time after time by others around them, and they do not see any good in their lives, or even life in general. This can be seen also in believers who truly have not developed faith and a healthy spiritual and mental outlook. We become a new creation in God's eyes when we follow Jesus, but many times this attitude or teachings are lost to the follower, due to lack of discipleship. A joyful heart should be evident in the church. Broken spirits should be healed one by one through developing healthy relationships. Do you mainly have a joyful heart about life, or do you let a broken spirit rule? The Lord wants you to have the joy in your heart, letting Him and others help you to overcome your negative thoughts and let joy fill your heart. Why? In Jesus we have hope, but you must choose to let Him give you this joy each day.

Prayer: Lord, help me each day to remember the reasons I should have a joyful heart. Give me the strength to avoid, or heal, a broken spirit. With your Spirit in me, my spirit can be healed. In your name, Amen

Personal Reflections: list the things that bring you a joyful heart in life, in your family, and in your church?

_____

_____

_____

_____

_____

_____

_____

_____

_____

_____

_____

_____

_____

_____

_____

_____

_____

_____

_____

_____

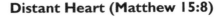

Distant Heart (Matthew 15:8)

"This people honors Me with their lips. But their heart is far from me."

What a sad commentary on the life of a religious person. Many believers think they're in a right relationship with God, but truly their hearts are far away from Him. They come to church each Sunday, or quite often, and sing praises to God. They may even listen to the preaching, but their hearts are not with Him. They have an appearance of being religious, but they are empty inside. They have knowledge, but not a heart relationship. This is what the gospels call the third seed. In the parable of the sower the third seed is one that takes root and looks like it is healthy. It looks like the right bush; it has the right leaves, in fact alongside all the others it looks no different, except for one thing. Other plants have fruit, but it does not. Bearing fruit shows it is healthy and viral. Without the fruit it is just taking up space. How many church goers are just taking up space and are barren of God's heart? Some may be deceived, and some are just deceivers themselves. I think for the most part many people truly think they are in a saving loving relationship with God when in fact they are not. Some just are deluded and use religion for their gain. What must happen for a bush to bear fruit? What must happen for a heart to be close to God? There must be true discipleship, true willingness to open and develop a heart for God that is void of religious jargon and rituals, and truly seek Him with all your heart. It is not a one-day-a week habit, but an everyday devotion to the One who loves you. Do you find yourself just going through the motions feeling empty inside? Do you go to church but never see any change or growth over the years? If so, go to your knees now, and everyday connect with the God of the universe, the God of love and relationships. Are you just paying lip service to God or do you truly have a heart that bears fruit?

Prayer: Lord, help my lips and my heart be one in my love for you. Search my heart and my motives to see that both are pure in your sight. In your name, Amen.

Personal Reflections: Honestly answer each question in the text. Share any fruit or growth in yourself you have seen over the years. If you find it hard to find any, then take time to wrestle with the text, truly repent, and become His following disciple of love.

_____

_____

_____

_____

_____

_____

_____

_____

_____

_____

_____

_____

_____

_____

_____

_____

_____

_____

_____

_____

Burning Heart. (Luke 24:32)

"They said to one another, "Were not our hearts burning within us while He was speaking to us on the road, while He was explaining the scripture to us?"

Although the two disciples did not know who was speaking to them on the road, their hearts still burned. The first truth here is that the Word of God itself has the power to burn hearts. What does it mean to have burning hearts? First, when one is on fire and excited about serving the Lord, then what you're hearing will drive you, and motivate you to act or believe. We cannot have one without the other. Second this burning heart could also be described as passion for what they were hearing. I think this is why many believers live a defeated and lackluster Christian life. They have no burning or passion in their heart. Some may have had it and let it subside, and others may have never had it, just living by tradition and not from a burning heart. Ask your heart, is it burning in any of these areas? If not, why not? Ask yourself, did I have passion for the Word, or did I let it be quince in my life? Then bow before the Father and pray for the burning of the Word and Spirit to come back. If you call yourself a believer and have never had any burning, then take a close look at your faith to see if you truly have a saving relationship with Jesus. The verse also goes on to tell us that the scripture was causing the burning in their hearts. What we see is that somewhere in the experience they were moved to this conviction, excitement, and passion. Wait, we too can explain it to others and have them burn when we do it with the leading of the Holy Spirit. The Word is powerful to the point of burning our hearts with passion of the scripture. What is Jesus speaking to you today? Does His voice touch and burn your heart to follow Him and His word? Just listen to Him on your road of life.

PRAYER: Oh, my Lord, burn my heart each day with conviction, excitement, and passion in my relationship with you and your word. Convict me, excite me. I know it must be my willingness to let you burn me with your passion. In Your name, Amen.

Personal Reflections: What things are you convicted of, excited about, and have passion for in God's kingdom?

_____

_____

_____

_____

_____

_____

_____

_____

_____

_____

_____

_____

_____

_____

_____

_____

_____

_____

_____

New Heart (Ezekiel 36:26)

Moreover, I will give you a <u>new heart</u> and put a new spirit within you, and I will remove the heart of stone from your flesh and give you a heart of flesh."

In context, God is speaking about what was going to come when the Spirit would be poured out, and a new covenant would be ushered in. In Ezekiel 18, He told His people to make a new heart in themselves. Both then and now God expects us to choose to change. We have the opportunity as disciples to have the Spirit dwell within us, and because of that presence God can work on our heart of stone and make it flesh. We can allow the Spirit to work in our lives or not. We still have control when He comes to dwell in our lives or we can spurn Him and not let Him do the complete work He is able and intend on doing in our lives. What is a new heart? A new heart is a new way of thinking. The heart is a depository of everything we have allowed in our lives. A new heart is evident in how we think about others, how we treat others, and how we look towards God in obedience and worship. The new heart will be realized in all these hearts in this book. Every positive heart you will study about and take to heart, and every negative heart you will hopefully recreate into a new heart. The problem is that we find it hard to keep the old heart at bay. It has been with us all these years and changing from an old heart to new one is an ongoing struggle even if we have the Spirit in us. The more the Spirit takes control of our lives, the more we can overcome the old way of thinking and doing. "Taking every thought captive" is an excellent way of developing a new heart. So, how is your new heart doing? Are you yielding to the Spirit so that your old heart is being replaced daily by the heart and Spirit of Jesus? If not, why not? When Christ enters our hearts, He gives us new life and ways of thinking and acting. What a wonderful life we will have as He makes us new creatures in heart and soul.

Prayer: Lord, create in me a new heart. Thank you for giving me a new heart through the power and work of your Spirit that is within me. I need and want you to help me. In Jesus' Name, Amen.

Personal Reflections: Since you became a disciple, what things are new in your heart? What other new things do you want to have in your heart?

_____

_____

_____

_____

_____

_____

_____

_____

_____

_____

_____

_____

_____

_____

_____

_____

_____

_____

_____

—

Humble Heart (Mathew 11:29)

"Take My yoke upon you and learn from me, for I am gentle and humble in heart, and you will find rest for your souls."

I have seen many a man that is the opposite of a humbled heart. I tried working with a preacher once in a Caribbean church, and for the first 15 days I heard nothing but how great he was as a preacher, intellect, and all-around know-it-all. There was nothing He claimed he could not do and do it better than anyone else. And everything he said he did in the church in the whole 21 days I was with him was void of God, there was no mention of God doing this work through him, but it was all about him. How sad it is for a man of God, or anyone taking credit for something they should give to God. A proud person has a hard, (if not impossible) time learning from someone else, because they can never take themselves out of the picture, or off the throne. Jesus said, "take my yoke and learn from me." Who else is better to learn from than Jesus? When you take all the credit for things then you take all the risk too, for when you take the credit you will not find rest for your souls. You will always be on call to stay perfect and live up to your boasting, and when you don't you will find yourself always striving to live up to your pride. What a burden to carry! It is the humble that God will lift up on the last day, and it will be the proud on this earth that will be humbled. There is no greater feeling than to hear another give their praise for what you do. But when you give your own praise there is an empty feeling as reward, and if one is looking to get praise from his own boasting or work then his reward is in his hand already, albeit a shadow of what God would have done if we were humble and gave Him all the credit. Have you taken His yoke and Humbled heart, or are you in control? Give Him his due and you will have eternal peace.

Prayer: Oh Lord, may I find rest in you. Help me to be as gentle and humble as Jesus. Let your heart be my heart in all I say and do. I want to learn from you daily. Teach me when I put myself above you and fail to give your Spirit the credit for all I am and all I do.

Personal Reflections: What things in the past week have you boasted about and taken credit for? List some things that you should give God credit for in your life.

_____

_____

_____

_____

_____

_____

_____

_____

_____

_____

_____

_____

_____

_____

_____

_____

_____

_____

_____

_____

Pondering Heart (Luke 2:19)

"But Mary treasured all these things pondering them in her heart."

Wow! Mary just heard the amazing things the shepherds had seen and heard about her newborn son. This added to her experience with the angel a few months before, causing her to think again of the magnitude of all that was happening. Just think, she was holding the firstborn of all fruits, the Savior of the world, the Lord of the universe, and the Creator of all. The honor bestowed upon her is unthinkable, and the responsibility she now has would be overwhelming, but at this point she treasured everything that was happening, pondering it in her heart. What does it mean to ponder in your heart? Ponder indicates weighing carefully in the mind something deeply and thoroughly. Meditation is to ponder. **What do you ponder about in your heart?** Or do you? Some people just go through life with their minds in neutral and do not think of the implications of their life and what can be. If you are a believer, then ponder this. Mary carried the Son of God, and how awesome that was, we also carry God in us. What do I mean? If you're a disciple, you have the Holy Spirit in you. You have God in you; that is awesome, that is something for each of us to treasure. Every day of our lives can potentially be wonderful. What do I mean "potentially?" We can quench or squander the opportunity to allow the Holy Spirit to fill us with His power and gifts. This includes giving us His character, so that others will look at us and see God. I hope you take the time to ponder what it means for God to continually go with you. Don't miss the chance to be filled; don't miss the chance to carry God in your heart. What does God have for you to do? Whatever He has for you is a wonderful thing to consider or ponder in your heart.

Prayer: Oh Lord, help me to ponder, moment by moment, your presence in my life. Let me not take it for granted that you come to live in me. Help me honor that by living a life pleasing to you. In your name, Amen.

Personal Reflections: Take time to ponder all this. Also, look at Ephesians 3:11-20 to see how the whole Godhead dwells in us.

_____

_____

_____

_____

_____

_____

_____

_____

_____

_____

_____

_____

_____

_____

_____

_____

_____

_____

_____

_____

_____

_____

_____

Pierced Heart (Acts 2:37)

"Now when they heard this, they were pierced to the heart, and said to Peter and the rest of the apostles, "Brethren, what shall we do?""

Pricked, pierced, or cut to heart are terms that indicate a severely convicted heart. Pierced is a term that shows a deep wound that could be fatal. In each of our lives our sinful, fleshly hearts are to die, and the only way is that we are pierced with a fatal wound. We are so convicted that we will want to come to the point that we say, "what must I do to go on living?" Four things lead to a pierced heart; the Word of truth, the touching of the Spirit, the open heart of the listener, and someone to proclaim the message. The Word is like a two-edged sword that pierces to the deepest part of the soul. It pierces at the same time as it heals. Like a surgeon's knife you must first cut out the bad so that the process of healing is possible. The same is true with our hearts; we must have the bad cut out. The second is the working of the Spirit. It takes the moving of the Spirit in a person's life to cause him to be pierced and come to his knees with conviction, Jesus will use the Word to make it happen. The third element is the listener. A person must be open to the truth spoken by God's messenger and yield to the touching of the Spirit to be pierced. The last, but not least, is the person who delivers the message. Romans 10 ask how will non-believers be able to listen, (or we could say be pierced and convicted) unless someone tells them? God could use the Word alone, but He chooses to use us to be a part of the process. How about you? Do you need to be pierced or convicted to follow Christ more deeply? Hopefully that happened when you began your journey. Are you willing to be God's messenger, a messenger that will help pierce someone's heart?

Prayer: Lord, each day pierce my heart so that I will come to you and hear what you have to say. Help me to listen to your Spirit and continually convict me of any wrong I may harbor in my heart. In Jesus name, Amen.

Personal Reflections: Think about your conversion. Were you pierced to the heart and convicted, or was it a sudden decision? Write times you can remember being pierced. What was your response?

_____

_____

_____

_____

_____

_____

_____

_____

_____

_____

_____

_____

_____

_____

_____

_____

_____

_____

_____

Cleansed Heart (Acts 15:9)

"And He made no distinction between us and them, cleansing their hearts by faith."

Let us parse this verse in context to see what is meant. "He," of course, is Jesus the Lord. "Us and them" are the Jews and Gentiles respectively. "Made no distinction" Is very important. The Jews have lived for thousands of years thinking they were the only ones God accepted. Now, this attitude is being brought over into Christianity and Paul is not going to stand for it. In Christ/Messiah there is no longer "us" and "them" it is all "we." There is neither Jew nor Gentile; we are all one in Christ spiritually. How does Paul tell us this is true? It comes with a cleansed heart by faith. You can have a proud Jewish person basking in being a chosen person, or a proud church going Gentile thinking they are the "new chosen" now at the replacement of the Jew. Both are dead wrong and are far from being cleansed hearts. We are saved because of this faith the Lord cleanses us. We can cleanse ourselves. Only God's power can do so based upon our faith and relationship with Him. It is not about our heritage, or being a part of the right church, but being in right relationship with the Lord. Are you cleansed by Jesus? If so, there will be no evidence of prejudice or pride towards any other person. Why should we boast except in our Lord? Our righteousness is as filthy rags; On our own we cannot cleanse our hearts no matter what we do, or no matter what church we belong to. Faith is the common response that brings us equally to the throne. To be cleansed of heart is to be pure and void of any stain in His eyes. Are you cleansed of heart by faith? This is all that matters. Everyone else must make that same choice, regardless of birth, race or association. I praise you Father for cleansing me and making me whole regardless of my past. My hope is in you. Thank you for making no distinction between the gentile or Jew, cleansing our hearts by faith.

Prayer: Lord, increase my faith that I may be continually cleansed by you. Help me Lord, not to look down on some, while also feeling inadequate to others in the faith. In Jesus' Name, Amen.

Personal Reflections: What things in your life need cleansing? What part of your faith that needs strengthened?

_____

_____

_____

_____

_____

_____

_____

_____

_____

_____

_____

_____

_____

_____

_____

_____

_____

_____

_____

Circumcised Heart (Deuteronomy 10:15, 16)

"Circumcise your hearts and be stiffened in your neck no longer."

What was the purpose of circumcision? It was for at least two reasons. One was for obedience's sake. That is, the covenant between God and man was sealed with this act of circumcision on the eighth day of a boy's life. It was also for sanitation sake. Most medical authorities think that there are fewer health problems when a man is circumcised. As with many other requirements in the wilderness they both had a health reason, and spiritual one between the Israelites and God. What was the symbolism behind this act? When the foreskin is removed, the male part is fully exposed. When the heart is circumcised then the heart is fully exposed. We see that God was serious when He commanded the Israelites to circumcise. He was even ready to kill those who did not obey Him. However, it is our choice to circumcise our hearts. We are to remove anything from our heart that is getting in the way of our devotion to God. Those who neglect or refuse to open their heart do so because of either being neglectful, stubborn, or stiff-necked towards God. Our faith is based upon a sincere heart toward God. Just saying a prayer or saying, "I believe" is no good if it does not come from the heart. God can tell the difference between verbiage and a circumcised heart. In the Old Testament only men were circumcised, but with the heart both men and women are to be circumcised in the heart. It is our choice to allow our hearts to be circumcised, and it is our choice to be stiff–necked or stubborn in our relationship with God. God wants us to be humble enough to be open and vulnerable with God, not stiff-necked and stubborn. When we are, Jesus will come in and show His unending love. Are you totally exposed to God?

Prayer: Lord, help me each day not to be stiff-necked; that is, help me not to be stubborn with my heart. Help me to open it in praise to you. Help me to remove anything that will block me from drawing closer to you. Amen.

Personal Reflections: What are things in your life that hinder your heart from being open to God? What do you have to do to circumcise your heart?

_____

_____

_____

_____

_____

_____

_____

_____

_____

_____

_____

_____

_____

_____

_____

_____

_____

_____

_____

_____

_____

Circumcised Heart two (Romans 2:29)

"But he is a Jew, who is one inwardly. And circumcision is that which is of the heart, by the Spirit, not by the letter and his praise is not from men, but from God."

As you learned in the previous passage circumcision is a spiritual act of the heart. In Paul's day, some Jewish leaders wanted to require the Gentile believers to be circumcised to become a follower of Jesus. Paul writes that it is no longer a requirement for the Gentile believer. In the First Covenant, God wanted the covenant to be one that is spiritual as it is now in the New Testament. This verse indicates that we all become Jews when we come to the Messiah. Now is not as physical or national importance, but spiritual. We become a part of Israel when we circumcise our hearts in a new covenant with God through Jesus/Yeshua. Remember we as Gentiles are grafted in, and that is an important fact for us and the ethnic Jew today. It is not by the letter of the law of old, but of the Spirit. The Holy Spirit comes and inwardly circumcises our heart. Just like parents circumcised the eight-day old boy, the Holy Spirit circumcises us the believer. He becomes our parent/guardian. But in this case, it is as a believer who wants it to happen. Circumcision is not from men with a knife, but it praises God it is from His Spirit. Circumcision of the heart is a supernatural event in each of our lives. It is usually as a part of repentance and yielding to God. Each of us must ask, have we allowed the Spirit to circumcise our heart? Have we asked Him to cut away the things that hinder total freedom in the Spirit? Have we allowed this transformation to make us different than before? If you are a Gentile, then rejoice that you now can be included in God's chosen people through the Spirit that makes both Jew and Gentile one in the flesh. If you're a Jew then you too must be circumcised of heart in the Spirit; it is not enough to be a Jew by the flesh, but by Spirit in Yeshua.

Prayer: Lord, my God, I come to yield my heart to be circumcised by your Spirit. Take away anything that gets in the way of my devotion to you. It is not by might, but by your Spirit that I can serve and love you from my heart. In Jesus' name, Amen.

Personal Reflections: List anything that gets in the way of your devotion to God. Meditate on whether you live by the letter of the law or the Spirit.

Sinking Heart (Gen. 42:28)

"Then he said to his brothers, 'My money has been returned and behold, it is even in my sack.' And their hearts sank, and they turned trembling to one another, saying what is this that God has done to us?"

Have you ever been in this situation? I have. I have been accused of something that I did not do or had any control over, but others thought I did. This kind of incidence is heart-breaking. It makes the heart drop to the floor so to speak, and you feel helpless. You begin to see all the implications of what might happen if this untruth is allowed to proceed. Your reputation, your job, or ministry might be diminished or taken away. Many times, in people's minds, one is guilty until proven innocent. That is not right, especially in the church. You may have even been set up in the process. The tendency is to get defensive, and rightly so, but that only seems to make things worse. It is hard enough to deal with the things you truly do wrong, and which should have consequences, but suffering for the things you did not do, or did with a good consciousness seems unfair at the time. We are living in a fallen world with fallen people, who at times want to test, and or destroy you if they can. Sometimes accidents just happen or with good intentions, we may have made a mistake about something. There are also times that Satan wants to accuse us falsely so as to knock us off balance or attempt to make us fall and react in a sinful way. But whatever the situation, God wants to see what we are made of and if we truly trust in Him in the times that our hearts sink. What Satan or others might have planned for us, God wants us to take each of those situations when our hearts sink. And to come to Him for comfort and wisdom for what to do, and how to react. Remember, "All things work out for those who love the Lord."

Prayer: My Lord, when I am falsely accused, help me to lean on you for understanding and patience. Help me to face my accusers with unwavering faith that you will see me through so that I may glorify you in my actions and attitudes. In your name, Amen.

Personal Reflections: Think of a time when you were falsely accused. How did you react? How did you cope? Would you do it differently now?

_____

_____

_____

_____

_____

_____

_____

_____

_____

_____

_____

_____

_____

_____

_____

_____

_____

_____

_____

Haughty Heart (Proverbs 18:12)

"Before destruction the heart of man is haughty, but humility goes before honor."

What is a haughty heart? A haughty heart is much like a proud heart but on steroids. It is obnoxious and outlandish and lets you know about it. It says, "look at me; I am the cat's meow." A proud heart can be hidden at times and does not necessarily expose itself to others, but a haughty heart is out there in your face. It wants you to know it is proud. It is proud to be proud. How do you think most people respond to a haughty heart? With disgust and dishonor? It is not a pretty picture to other people's eyes. Usually, people turn away and get fed up with such a person. The thing a haughty heart yearns for is recognition, but it is thwarted by its haughtiness. The logical conclusion to such a person is destruction. This person is so hooked on themselves that they self-destruct, or by their action, cause others to pull away and destroy their relationships or future endeavors. And most of all, God hates a haughty heart because He does not get the glory. God will not honor such a person; rather, He will take any protection from that person and let him fall. At best God will not honor him with any accolades and be assured God's honoring is better than anything we could hope for. Have you ever had a haughty heart? If so, then repent and realize that who you are or can be is because God has created you with such potential and abilities. A fool that has a haughty heart, a haughty heart that is bound to fail and fall. If you do, then the only hope is to look to the One, who has given you all that you have and are. Humility will serve you best in this life. Even if you do not have a haughty heart, you may at times have had a proud one. Do not be fooled, this attitude will lead to one that is haughty. The answer to destruction, of course, is humility in the presence of God. God will honor those who know that God is in control.

Prayer: Lord, help me to be honest with myself and others, and not have a haughty heart that boasts of who and what I am at the expense of my relationships with You and others. In your name.

Personal Reflections: List some things you have been proud or haughty about. What was the outcome? What should be your attitude?

Searched Heart (Romans 8:27)

"And He who searches the hearts knows what the mind of the Spirit is, because He intercedes for the saints according to the will of God."

Who is He? It is most assuredly the Holy Spirit that searches our heart to see who we truly are and what we need. This is true to the extent He is dwelling in us. That, of course, comes from the promise of being His disciple and obeying Acts 2:38. Due to the indwelling of the Holy Spirit we have his presence in our lives. Who knows us best, warts and all? It is, of course, those who live with us daily. Does the Spirit of God live with us daily? Do we make Him a part of our lives? Do we listen when he speaks? We are fools when we do not listen and follow the leading of the Holy Spirit. I see two important facts here that we need to understand. First, God searches our hearts and knows each person. We are an open book to Him. Therefore, we must ask what is in our heart. Would you want your next-door neighbor or even best friend to know what is truly in your heart on a day to day basis? Or do you hide your true self? Do you really know what is in your heart, or do you hide it from yourself and rationalize who you truly are? We cannot hide our true heart from God. He knows all and sees all, so let us stop playing games with Him and ourselves and be honest. Secondly, is a great blessing for each child of God. We have the Spirit as our intercessor who personally goes to the Father in the will of God. That is, each of us can and should be in the will of God because we have the Spirit that knows us better than we know ourselves, and, therefore, looks out for our best interest. If our heart is right then, He will keep us in the will of God. What is God's will for your life? Amazingly most believers/disciples do not even ask or search for God's will daily, some never do. Last, we must praise God for His provision. The Spirit knows our need, and we can rest assured our needs will be met if we allow Him to work in our lives.

Prayer: Lord, search me and help me to be true to you and myself in all things. Help me to be within your will and reveal to me each day your will for my life.

Personal Reflections: Ask yourself two questions; What is in my heart? What is God's will for my life today and long term?

_____

_____

_____

_____

_____

_____

_____

_____

_____

_____

_____

_____

_____

_____

_____

_____

_____

_____

_____

_____

_____

Hardened heart two (Exodus 4:21)

"And the Lord said to Moses, 'when you go back to Egypt see that you perform before Pharaoh all the wonders which I have put in your power, but I will harden his heart so that he will not let the people go."

This event has always been somewhat of a puzzle to me. Why did God harden Pharaoh's heart? One can postulate about the reason. One can just accept it without question or curiosity, but then we would have to cut this portion a bit short. And we could just ignore it altogether. In God's sovereignty, we could just let God be God and think this is what He wanted at this point. First, of all we need to start with God's foreknowledge and trust that He knew Pharaoh was going to continue to resist, and he decided to use his attitude to further His intended will that needed to take place so that the deliverance could be realized. I do not want to be in a position for God to harden my heart. For God to want to harden me, I first must be in a state of disobedience, or worse, fallen from grace, or have never been under grace to begin with. God will use us one way or the other to fulfill His will. We will either be a vessel of honor or dishonor. That is; the potter will have his way in order to accomplish His will. The vessel of honor will be a person who follows the Lord and is used for the good of the kingdom. God has promised us that nothing will be too hard for us to bear. The vessel of dishonor will be on the other side of God's people and will be used to fulfill His will as a negative pawn. For example, we see that Judas is the prime example of all time. He was a son of the devil, the Bible states. God did not make him that way or kept him that way; God just knew his heart and therefore used him in His plan. He also will use you to do His will, so be sure to be on the right side of that will so that God will not choose to harden your heart. If you have a relationship with God and His Spirit you will never have to worry.

Prayer: Lord, please use me as you see best for your kingdom's work. Keep my heart soft in your presence and not hard towards your will and commandments.

Personal Reflections: Is there anything in your heart that seems God may have used your heart for His purpose? What can you do to be sure your heart does not become hardened?

_____

_____

_____

_____

_____

_____

_____

_____

_____

_____

_____

_____

_____

_____

_____

_____

_____

_____

Fools Heart (Psalm 14:1)

"The fool has said in his heart, 'There is no God' They are corrupt, they have committed abominable deeds. There is not one who does good."

You may say as you read this, "I am no fool, I have not said, "there is no God. I believe, so why should I read this?" To reach those who say, there is no God, you must know what it means to be in their shoes. All of us at times have our battles but let us never become fools. Have you felt society is becoming more de-synthesized to the things of God? I remember in the early 60's, watching TV and growing up in an innocent world of Mayberry, My Three Sons, and "well you just don't talk about those kinds of things world." I was young and did not realize that from the beginning people either shook their finger at God or did not believe he existed. At the heart of this discussion are people's eternal lives. It is one thing not to follow God, but it is hopeless when one does not believe God exists at all. What else is at stake when one does not believe? Our whole fabric of society is at stake concerning the existence of God. With no God, you have lawlessness, you have the disrespect for human life and dignity, and you have hopelessness. A person with no God is a person who has no future in the after-life. Why is a person a fool that does not believe there is a God? Simply, there is so much proof of our God that it is foolish to believe otherwise. He is a fool that sees the evidence and does not accept it. The fool that rationalizes away this proof by wanting to look away. If there is no God, then the door is open to irresponsibility and total selfishness. "There is no one that does good" refers to the atheist in his depravity, not to the Spirit-filled believer. You may say, "I know of atheists that do-good things." Maybe, but their result will be corrupt in the end. A society based on atheism and agnosticism will degrade eventually to a lawless society, at least in the way it treats others. Look at Stalin who said: "if there is no God, then mankind is just an animal to do with any way you wish. If they are in your way, put them away even if they are your kind. Do we who believe there is a God live like there is not one. Yes, and that is even worse. To know and do otherwise brings more judgment upon themselves than those who don't. Praise be to God who shows us His truth in His love and creation.

Prayer: Lord, I pray no one ever calls me a fool. Lord, help me always to honor your existence with my life and dedication. You are my God protect me from my flesh so that I will honor you always. In Your name, Amen.

Personal Reflections: What attitudes and actions in your life might show others you do not believe in God? What things might you say to an atheist to prove there is a God?

_____

_____

_____

_____

_____

_____

_____

_____

_____

_____

_____

_____

_____

_____

_____

_____

_____

_____

_____

_____

God looks at Heart (1 Samuel 16:7)

"... For God sees not as man sees, for man looks at the outward appearance, but the Lord looks at the heart."

This is so true. God sees all kinds of things that man does not. Let us make this personal; for God sees not as Michael Householder sees. Put your name in there too. How do we look at the outward appearance? Each of us has been at the end of peoples' judgments of us. And even our judgment of ourselves can be wrong. This is the main point here, man judges from the outside, but God judges from the inside. Man sees our mistakes, our sins, our idiosyncrasies, our quirks, our weird personality, but not our true self most of the time. Some people come across as smooth talkers; you know, the proverbial lawyers and used-car salesman. I do not know why new car salesmen are left out. But you get the point. Sometimes these people try to make things look good that in reality are not good for you. Let me give another example. I have had, from time to time, cold sores inside my mouth and let me tell you it is painful and makes your whole body and countenance look abysmal. I have had people judge me as being stuck up or grumpy, but in fact I was in pain. Many people have outside abnormalities but have the greatest hearts in the world. The only way to know this is to look inside and get to know them. What God does, for He knows that every outside appearance is temporary and it is what is in the heart that is true and genuine about a person. The heart or soul that will produce lasting results and determines the true person, either as a bad person or good one. We even look on our outside and judge ourselves wrongly. This also speaks to the person that claims to be a believer. A person can look great and speak great but be dead inside. God knows this and usually the person will be found out in the long run. Be honest with God and yourselfs for your heart depends on it.

Prayer: Lord, please show me my true heart as you see it. Let others too, see my true heart, as I am honest with them and myself. In your name I pray amen.

Personal Reflections: : What are some things on your outside that you have judged yourself with? Have you or someone else said you or I am ugly or stupid. List some, then tell yourself your value is your heart set on God, not what you and others think. Pray and list things that are good in your heart.

_____

_____

_____

_____

_____

_____

_____

_____

_____

_____

_____

_____

_____

_____

_____

_____

_____

_____

Bribed Heart   (Ecclesiastics 7:7)

"For oppression makes a wise man mad. And a bribe corrupts the heart."

What is a bribe? In Biblical terms, it is nothing more than "an in - your-face" temptation. A bribe is inherently wrong. A bribe starts with a proposition. If you do this, I will do this, if you do not do it then this will happen to you. If you want a better life or more money than you are getting, then do this for me. Look at what you can get if you will only help me this once, or if you look away for a moment and let me by I will give you this in return. A good man with a good heart can be bribed if there is enough benefit for him to do so. Is this true or false? Is this true in your life? Has it ever happened to you? Let us look at two examples. The first bribe was of Eve. She was given a proposition that she felt she couldn't refuse. It was of course based in selfishness, and not altruism or trust. If your standards and commitment level to what is right is strong enough, then you will refuse the bribes in your life. But if not then you will succumb to temptations. The second bribe was to Jesus. He was bribed by Satan the great briber of all, as was Eve. But Jesus saw the whole picture. He knew what was offered was not in the end worth the risk and the result of taking the bribe. That is the shortcoming of most of us we do not see the whole picture. We see the benefit in the moment but fail to weigh the consequences of the choice. The heart is corrupted when you are asked to do something that you know is wrong and then you yield to the temptation. Rationalization is the process in your decision. One must rationalize, "It can't be that bad. See all the good things I can get, or do with the money or power? Where are you in the bribe-o-meter? How much of a momentary benefit would it take for you to take a bribe? Or, do you see the big picture that always following the right path is the best path? When you see what the Lord has in store for each follower, a bribe is a mere cloud.

Prayer: Lord, help me to be by your side and study your Word daily so that when bribes come I will see the whole picture and lean on you for understanding. In your name I do pray. Amen

Personal Reflections: Be honest. What would make you take a bribe? Think about the things that you will make a stand on. List the things that may tempt you to take a bribe.

_____

_____

_____

_____

_____

_____

_____

_____

_____

_____

_____

_____

_____

_____

_____

_____

_____

Tablets of human heart (2 Corinthians 3:3)

"…being manifested that you are a letter of Christ cared for by us written not with ink, but with the Spirit of the living God, not on tablets of stone, but on tablets of human hearts."

What a declaration! We are letters of Christ'. We are the material that He is writing on. In the Old Testament, God wrote on tablets of stone, very impersonal and non-relational. Once written on stone words could not be changed or written on again. The age of grace gave us a God that wants to have a relationship with us through Christ. The Father wanted relationships also in Old Testament times but the Israelites kept rejecting Him. Now He speaks to us through the heart, with Christ as the author of our faith. Any book is valid based upon its author. Jesus writes on our hearts with the Spirit and not ink. Ink can fade away, but what the Spirit imprints on our hearts is for eternity. What is the difference between stone and heart? One is inanimate, and one is alive. You can choose to have a heart of stone or a human heart. You can choose to allow the Spirit to write on your heart. If you do, then He will write your legacy, your story of His life with you; a story that is filled with life and worth. He will give you the instructions on how to live and follow the Father. What does it mean on human hearts? It means we are special. We are not animals; we have hearts created in His image, to have His image imprinted upon our hearts. When someone reads our hearts they should be able to see God as the author and not us. The question is He has written on your heart, or have you not allowed Him to make a difference in your life? To write on your heart is the same as changing your heart. Are you writing a new story, a different story than you have written for yourself. With God's Spirit you can be a best seller instead of irrelevant paperback. Paul was so proud of those who followed Jesus through his ministry. What will the Spirit write on your heart.

Prayer: Lord, thank you for writing on my heart. Help me to allow it more each day and give me the heart to follow your way. In Your precious name, from day to day Amen.

Personal Reflections: What things have you written on your heart that you want erased? What things has he written so far and what do you want to be written on your heart?

_____

_____

_____

_____

_____

_____

_____

_____

_____

_____

_____

_____

_____

_____

_____

_____

_____

_____

_____

_____

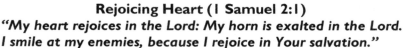

Rejoicing Heart (I Samuel 2:1)
"My heart rejoices in the Lord: My horn is exalted in the Lord. I smile at my enemies, because I rejoice in Your salvation."

The heart is the seat of affections, and emotional expression is at its most healthful when it rejoices. Hanna had just received a blessing birth of her son. She had a rejoicing heart. A heart that cannot feel the joy of triumph in God's glory is a sad, defeated heart. When we realize what Hannah declares in verse two, then we too should have a heart that rejoices and feels triumphal because the one who we serve is our rock. No one is as holy or can stand beside Him. The world needs to see, even our fellow brothers and sisters in Christ need to see, that we have a rejoicing heart toward God no matter what circumstances. The believer should be able to look beyond this world and our present existence and find a reason for rejoicing. In this text, Hannah sees that in salvation. This is not all that there is, even though at times it may seem like it is so. Can we find a reason to rejoice in everything? Have you ever had attacks from the enemy, Satan, or even other fleshly enemies? I sure have. I have even had so called brothers and sisters who have become enemies due to their evil intentions towards me. I surely had a hard time rejoicing when I was under attack. Why should I rejoice even during trials and conflict? I know in the scheme of things this life is not all there is. I know where my salvation comes from. I know in whom I trust. Therefore, I can rejoice in my heart, I can smile at my enemies because in Him I am free to exalt and rejoice. Think of all the things you should rejoice about. Think about what grace has done to give you joy. Rejoice in your relationship with Christ your Lord. Rejoice because of your salvation

Pray: Lord, may I have a rejoicing heart and exalt you with my heart, even in times that seem hard. Fill my heart with rejoicing. Help me to see you in your greatness. Forgive me when I do not rejoice in you as I should. Help me see all the reasons to rejoice. Help me to name them, to claim them and to rejoice in you always.

Personal Reflections: What things in your life can you look at and see a reason to rejoice? What situations seem hard to rejoice in that I could have a reason to rejoice?

_____

_____

_____

_____

_____

_____

_____

_____

_____

_____

_____

_____

_____

_____

_____

_____

_____

_____

Troubled Heart 2 (Proverbs 25:20)

"Like one who takes off a garment on a cold day, or like vinegar on soda is he who sings songs to a troubled/heavy heart."

This is a very brilliant example of what happens to most of us at certain times in our lives. For some people it is a lifestyle, and to others it is a passing event. What do I mean? First, most people don't take off a coat on a cold day. The result is not a desired outcome. Second, pouring vinegar on soda destroys both, again, an undesired result. Now let us look at a person who has a troubled or heavy heart. We all have one at times. In this state a trite remedy of singing a song does not work; it may even insult the person having the troubled heart. Each of us has different personalities, and approaches situations differently. A person with jovial personality may think, "if I sing a song it may cheer the person up." Some people with a troubled heart wants others to suffer right along with them, or at least hope that they will sympathize with them in their down trodden feelings. However, some people live to feel bad. That is, they would not be happy if they were not troubled. Sometimes they act like this is the only way they can get any attention. This is sad and not normal. Most of us, from time to time go through a troubled/heavy heart in life. Things just don't go right, or circumstances bring us down because we are living in the human condition. Sometimes life just happens, and it is not pretty. In a circumstance like this then yes, we would hope others would be sensitive in our troubled heart. And if others react to our songs then minister, but never let it bring you down to the point that you lose your song in your heart. Listen, love, and console, but do not be co-dependent. When we do have a troubled heart then know that it is in Christ that you have hope in a God that knows what you need. But it does not stop with God. Each of us must try to be sensitive to others and their troubled hearts. For someday soon you may need an understanding heart in your time of need.

Prayer: Lord, help me to be sensitive to others needs as I hope they will to me. Lord I trust that no matter what happens I have you to help me through. In your name I pray dear Father.

Personal Reflections: What troubles your heart today? Whom can you go to who truly listens in your times of trouble? Do you find yourself often having a troubled or heavy heart? If so, what can you do about it?

_____

_____

_____

_____

_____

_____

_____

_____

_____

_____

_____

_____

_____

_____

_____

_____

_____

_____

Honest heart (Luke 8:15)

"But the seed in the good soil, these are ones who have heard the word in an <u>honest</u> and good heart, and hold it fast, and bear fruit with perseverance."

The first thing in this passage that is different from the previous seed that the seed is the same. The seed is the work of the Spirit or God's Word in a person's life. The first three seeds rejected the prompting of the Spirit. Second, we see that there is "good soil." The other soils were not good and not willing to accept the seed. Next, we see two conditions to receive the seed. First, the heart must be honest, honest in admitting they are a sinner and willing to let the seed take root. What kind of fruit does an honest heart bring? The fruit of righteousness, the fruit of good deeds, and the fruit of the Spirit. An honest heart is one that is real to God and self. A disciple of Christ must admit his sin and fault and therefore making the first step to eradicating both in his life. When sin is gone or minimized, then growth can blossom or bear fruit. When you are in denial, or not honest with oneself, then you will think you are okay, when you are truly not, therefore no fruit will come in and through your life. A true disciple is one that is honest. For honesty leads to repentance and repentance leads to the fruit of salvation. You must ask do I have an honest heart before God and myself, if not, I have no relationship either. Second, we see that the heart is good and ready to allow the seed to bear fruit. But the first thing that must happen is that the heart must be willing to hear the message of the seed. Most who do not want to hear with the honest heart. Now it is not a onetime event, but rather each of us must hold fast and be faithful to the end. Lastly, continue to bear fruit with faithfulness and perseverance. All this, of course, must continually be based in an honest heart. The honest heart will be open to allowing God to work in their life on a daily basis. Be honest with yourself and with God, and then God will make you fruitful.

Prayer: Lord, help me be honest with you and myself that I may bear much fruit in my life and for your kingdom. In Christ, Amen.

Personal Reflections: What things in your life have you not been honest with to God, to self, and to others? Pray for honesty and think of examples to be honest in each of these areas and relationships.

_____

_____

_____

_____

_____

_____

_____

_____

_____

_____

_____

_____

_____

_____

_____

_____

_____

_____

_____

One Heart (Ezekiel 11:19)

"And I shall give them one heart, and shall put a new spirit within them..."

One of the most frequent and damaging things that went on with the children of Israel were their times of division. The children of Israel gives us many examples of division. Starting with the sons of Abraham, and continuing with David and Saul, the 12 men who spied on Canaan, and 12 tribes and the two kingdoms, and on and on. In each case God's will and kingdom suffered, but the people suffered the most. Throughout the Old Testament it is evident that God never gave up on Israel as a whole. God's desire was and is, that His people have one heart. Ezekiel was charged with telling the wayward people that there will be a time that they will be called and brought back to their homeland. And most important they would be given one heart. When a fellowship or people are one in heart, then nothing can stop them from growing and being fruitful in God's eyes. It is in division that the world mocks at the people of God and turns it's back on Him. When those who call themselves His children bicker, argue, and fight, then damage is done in the body or relationship. The conflict is usually over silly selfish things. Jesus prayed that His disciples would continue as a unified body. Unity is still His desire for all of us today. What does it mean to be one? One in purpose, one in following God, one in love, yes, these are some places to start. If we cannot be one in love and in following God, then we do not have much of a foundation to build upon in our christian walk. The first place to start is one in heart with God in a discipling relationship. Being a Christ follower is not a one-time statement of "I believe," but a life of getting to know Him on an intimate basis. To become one with someone is to know that person so deeply that both of you know the thoughts and intents of their being, to the point of congruence inasmuch as possible. Are you one with God? If not, why not?

Prayer: Lord, help me get out of the way and focus on knowing you more and more so that we can become one in the body of Christ. In Jesus name, amen.

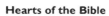

Personal Reflections: Reflect on what you must do to become one with Jesus. To do so you have to give up what it is that divides you and Him.

Fearing heart (Deuteronomy 5:29)

"Oh, that they had such a heart in them, that they would fear me, and keep all my commandments always, that it may be well with them and with their sons forever."

Does anyone like to be fearful? Is a loving God a God we must fear? Let us first think about "fear" in the biblical sense. Some say the fear is a sense of awe, not being afraid of a loving God, for God would not want us to fear Him. We should have a sense of awe towards God, but awe or fear is more than that. God is an awesome God that does require our respect, but at the same time demands a sense of fear. God is a God of judgment and with a potential of judgment comes a fear of being on the wrong side of judgment. Jonathan Edwards preached. "We should be concerned about being "in the hands of an angry God." God is angry with sin and sinners alike. Some say, oh no, He is only angry at sin, but He loves the sinner. Why would He condemn those who sin? Because He must. Yes, he does love all His creation, but this does not shield those who sin from His anger and should not back off when people need know this side of the God almighty. I think all the ideas of fear fit that God is a just and loving God. In this passage, God wants to relay that His people's hearts should be one that has a fear to the point of keeping the commandments because of the consequences from a just God. The important fact is that we are not saved by obeying commandments, but rather by following the one who commanded them. If we are to have a heart for the author of the commandments, then should our heart not rejoice in obeying what He commanded? If not, then maybe our heart is not one that is after the Lord, after all, that person should still have some fear. Perfect love casts out fear, but I say perfect love obeys the perfect lover, Jesus. Sometimes fear keeps you obeying the law of the land, so should your obedience be toward Christ's commands. If you love me, you will obey me, if not, then is your faith a saving faith? This verse ends with a promise that God will be with those who obey.

Prayer: Lord, help me to respect your commandments, for in doing so I respect and love you. In Your name I pray, Amen.

Personal Reflections: List the two kinds of fear we talked about. Example: The fear of the dark is unproductive. Fear of putting your hand in the fire, productive.

_____

_____

_____

_____

_____

_____

_____

_____

_____

_____

_____

_____

_____

_____

_____

_____

_____

_____

_____

_____

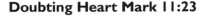

Doubting Heart Mark 11:23

"Truly I say to you, whoever says to this mountain, be taken up and cast into the sea, and does not doubt in his heart, but believes that what he says is going to happen it shall be granted him."

Wow, this is so awesome, but so unbelievable to most of us, even we who call ourselves Christians. Move a mountain, who really believes this statement literally? Most would consider this statement to be is figurative or spiritualized, but not truly possible. Jesus was trying to make a point of how their faith was not big enough, but did He mean it? Is it possible for a living creator God to move His own creation? Did He stop the wind and sea? Did He restore the hands, ears, and eyes of the leper from nothing to something brand new? Of course, we must say yes, or we say we lack faith, and we would not want to admit to that. How would others think of us? Let us be frank. We do have little faith when it comes to the power of God in our lives. We know Jesus did all these things and more, but can that transfer over to our lives in real time? How big is our heart? Is it big enough to move mountains? How often should we move mountains in our wife? I do not have all the answers, but I have seen God work in powerful ways in my life. What more could He do if I had no doubt in my heart. A person who has seen a miracle of God has a hard time explaining that experience to another who has not experienced it. He must believe in faith that person is truly relaying what happened. Where is your heart? Is it weak and doubting, or is it strong in faith that God can do great things through your life? We will never know the capacity of our heart to believe until we step out and open up to God's power to move in and through us. He has promised, do we trust and believe? Take a step today without a doubting heart.

Prayer: Lord, I need you every day to help my unbelief to change into belief in your power. All that I am and can do is in your power and through my faith. Lord, I trust your power, but not my faith. Help me trust you Lord. In Your holy name, Amen.

Personal Reflections: Write down an event when you think God showed a miracle in your life. Write down a time you doubted, and God showed you His power instead. What things do you need to do in order to trust more and not doubt?

_____

_____

_____

_____

_____

_____

_____

_____

_____

_____

_____

_____

_____

_____

_____

_____

_____

Returning heart (Jeremiah 24:7)

"...I will be their God, for they will <u>return</u> to Me with their whole heart."

At the beginning of this verse, God had given the children of Israel a heart to know Him. When people know God they are motivated to return to Him. What does it mean, "return?" First, the Israelites had come to God and gone from him many times, and they returned again and again over the years. When a person see that God is their God, then they will return and follow again. But, there are conditions. The return must be preceded with a whole heart. Not a sense of pacifying God, but genuine returning with a repentant heart. Sorrow and change are involved in repentance. There must be a turning or returning from somewhere if you are to repent from your past. If you are returning to God, then it must involve your turning away from that which enticed you away in the first place; the love of the world, or the selfishness of your soul. Many believers have started with the Lord but have begun to fall away and go back to their old lifestyle, or friends. When they again get to know God, hopefully, they will return to God. The prodigal son comes to mind as an example. Have you been a prodigal son or daughter? If so return to your first love with your whole heart. If you know of a prodigal pray for them to return. We can also apply this to those who have never followed Jesus as disciples. You should be challenged first to begin to know God in a fundamental sense. When someone introduces knowledge about God, then the Holy Spirit can touch that heart, and have a chance now to turn to Him, both in repentance and commitment as a disciple. Second answer to man's return is found in Jerimiah 29:11. When a person calls on God, comes and prays to Him, then He will listen, heal, and restore that person to faith. Who in your life needs to return?

Prayer: Lord, show me the ways I have turned from you. Show me so that I may return to you in every way of my life with my whole heart. If I know anyone who needs to turn, then give me the opportunity and words to help them. In your name I pray, Amen

Personal Reflections: What ways have you turned, or returned, to God? What do you still need to do so that you commit with your whole heart?

_____

_____

_____

_____

_____

_____

_____

_____

_____

_____

_____

_____

_____

_____

_____

_____

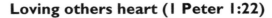

Loving others heart (1 Peter 1:22)

"Since you have in obedience to the truth purified your souls for a sincere love of the brethren, fervently love one another from the heart."

How do we love one another? In this passage, there are two main things to consider in our love for our fellow brothers and sisters in Christ. The first thing is to have a sincere love for our fellow brothers. How easy is it to be insincere in your affections towards someone? Unfortunately, it is very easy for some. Think about your relationships. Are you always honest and sincere in your love towards your fellow brothers in Christ? Or do you find yourself not being honest with others about your feelings? As disciples, we are expected to love one another in the church, even if we do not feel like or want to. The word "love" in the Greek is "agape" that is a Godly love. To naturally love this way is hard, and we need God's influence to give us power to have this kind of love towards our brethren. God will not help if we are not sincere about our love, it then is not true love but a fake one from other motives. The second thing God tells us is to have a <u>fervent</u> love for one another. A love that is strong and vibrant. To truly show your love, it must come from the heart. If it does, then it will be easy to be fervent about it. That is; you must choose to be fervent. It is very hard to fake a passionate love because you will have to be a real good actor to fake that type of love. How can we have this kind of love? Each of us must realize that we cannot do it on our own. Before you can truly love another, you must purify your souls in obedience to the truth. Each one should ask, "obedience to what?" the truth revealed in God through Jesus. Since He first loved us, we then should love one another. Love is the only way the world will see Jesus in us. Will someone see Him today?

Prayer: Lord, help me to love as You have loved me. Help me to be honest with my love for others and to be fervent in my love to my brothers. Love is not mere verbal declarations but be loving in your actions for the demonstration of your love for me.

Personal Reflections: What have you done this week to show your love to others? Think of what you can do to show you love to three people this week. What can you do to show your Love to God?

_____

_____

_____

_____

_____

_____

_____

_____

_____

_____

_____

_____

_____

_____

_____

_____

_____

_____

_____

_____

Joyless heart (Lamentations 5:15)

"The joy of our heart has ceased. Our dancing has been turned into mourning."

Have you ever been in a hopeless state of mind? I dare say that some of my readers have not; others can say yes of course I have; and even others may say I am in that state at this moment. Take a real look at this whole book, the children of Israel have lost everything they hold dear. The captors have taken everything and have put them in bondage. What they used to take for granted now they have to pay for. Their freedom is gone and so are their hearts desires. When a people have no control over their lifes then hopelessness is a common outcome. In some instances people have everything they need, and still have no joy in their mind or heart. It may be easier to have joy when you have all your needs have been taken care of, but I have found that is not always true. I have seen materially pour people who are full of joy, and I have seen some very well provided for people joyless. Is joy more a state of mind or perspective? Paul says, "I can be content in whatever state I am in." Why? Because he knew his circumstances were temporary. He had hope in what was to come, what was promised through his relationship with Jesus. In many cases, we put ourselves in hard times due to our choices and rebellions, so should not blame God. We have no excuse but must repent and turn again to God. "What we sow we reap." In some cases we are placed in situations through no cause of our own, but God allows it so that we can more deeply depend on Him. In all cases, we need to depend on the Lord by believing His promise, "I will never leave you nor forsake you." In all things rejoice in the Lord always, it is a Spirit filled state of mind. Look up, and dance again; rejoice again; for in Christ we should live and have our being. If you know someone who needs to dance again, be there to show him/her the joy in your heart. Go forth, dance, sing, and rejoice.

Prayer: Lord, help those that are a hopeless state. Show them your love and mercy. Let us come to you with joy and dancing even if all seems hopeless now. In You, I base my hope. Amen

Personal Reflections: Where are you? Are you one who is always complaining and have no joy in your life? Are you going through a time of depression and sadness due to some current events? If so, take some time and list some good things in your life.

_____

_____

_____

_____

_____

_____

_____

_____

_____

_____

_____

_____

_____

_____

_____

_____

_____

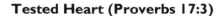

Tested Heart (Proverbs 17:3)

"The refining pot is for silver and the furnace is for gold, but the Lord tests the hearts."

The silver and gold are tested by fire. The Smith starts with the nuggets and rocks to see what the quality of the ore is. The gold is heated to the point that all the impurities are burned away. Pure silver and gold will not burn away, but the dross will. The ore is being tested to see what it's worth. The same is the case with the heart in God's hand. He test our hearts to see what dross is and what is the pure part of our heart. Sadly, in some cases the ore is cast aside because very little precious metal is produced. A good silversmith can tell right off if any good come from the ore. The same is true with our heart in God's hands. First, each of us must ask how our purity is in the sight of the Lord. Second, what test will have to be made to see our worth? We are told that when we go before the Lord we will see what has been burned away and what will last for eternity. If we tell a white lie, get angry, or do anything, not in the reverence of the Lord then we produce dross. If we fail to change our mindset, our lifestyle, or our direction in life and not follow the Lord daily, then we are producing dross. If we fail to love others, ourselves, and God with all our hearts, then we produce dross in our lives. At the end of our days what have we done to produce gold in our lives? Our purity, though, is not based on what we do alone, but in whom we become. We must become like God in everything we say and do. The only way we can do that is to develop our relationship with Jesus in love and honor. If we do that, then we will likewise treat others as Jesus would. What will last is who we become and who we touch for Him in the process. Each day may have its test of how much gold you will produce? Right now you have a chance to produce more silver and gold each day that you live for Him.

Prayer: Lord, please burn away any impurity in my life. Help me to be pure in your sight. Lord, show me the things I need to do to show forth your greatness.

Personal Reflections: What things in you produce dross? How have you seen God test you in the past week to see if your made of gold or dross?

_____

_____

_____

_____

_____

_____

_____

_____

_____

_____

_____

_____

_____

_____

_____

_____

_____

_____

_____

Obedient Heart (Romans 6:17)

But thanks be to God that though you were slaves of sin, you became obedient from the heart to that form of teaching to which you were committed."

Jesus said, "if you obey me you show your love for me." Why is love and an obedient heart tied together? One difference between a believer and a non-believer is that a non–believer has no will or desire to obey God, or His commandments. If that is the case, God will not save that person. Satan believes there is a God, but he does not obey. Now it is understood that a non-believer does not believe nor obey what God says to do in His Word, and we should not expect them to until they make a commitment to follow Jesus as a disciple. What about people who call themselves believers and do not obey God? I see three things in this passage. First, we were slaves to sin. That is, we were obedient to our sinning. We were obedient to our selfish ways, and the ways of the world. Second, we became committed, or should have to Jesus as Lord and the teachings He and the Spirit laid out in the Word. Because of this commitment to leave sin and be obedient from the heart to the teachings of Christ, we were no longer slaves to sin. Third, you cannot be a committed believer and at the same time be a slave to sin. If you call yourself a believer and still have not changed your lifestyle you may never have truly committed to Him and His teachings, and therefore will not be obedient to them. If you are reading this and know in your heart that your commitment was shallow, then go to God in faith and truly commit to be following disciple. If you do not commit to follow, then believing is not enough. If you truly believe you will follow and obey from the heart the teachings that Christ and the Word give you. If you have made the commitment then continue your obedience to the end, and He will reward you.

Prayer: Lord, help me to be committed to you with an obedient heart, not just with lip service, but with action in changing my life through obedience in your Word. In Your name, amen.

Personal Reflections: Think of three things you need to obey in God's word.

_____

_____

_____

_____

_____

_____

_____

_____

_____

_____

_____

_____

_____

_____

_____

_____

_____

_____

Blameless Heart (2 Chronicles 15:17)

"But the high places were not removed from Israel. Nevertheless Asa's heart was blameless all his days."

In the midst of temptation Asa resisted following everyone else in worshiping other gods; he was blameless before God. What does it mean to be blameless? It does not mean Asa was sinless, but that in his heart he kept himself directed in the right place. His motives and life wre focused on God and not those who were following other so-called gods. He knew whom he served and continued unwavered in his commitment even when most others did not. Can you say you are blameless before God in this way? Can you say when others are going the way of the world that you stand firm and do not waver in your commitment to follow God as His disciple, or do you get swayed by the temptations of the world and enticement of others around you? It is hard in an ever-increasing evil world when everything, but Christian is praised, and Christianity has become a liability. What do you do when there are high places in your surroundings? What must you do to keep blameless in heart? You first must keep your heart pure. Stay away from participating in those things that may bring you down. When we go back to our old ways, then we can again be soiled by their influence. In 2 Peter 1:5-8 we see encouragement to add to our faith several qualities to help us stay focus on God. First thing is to keep growing in the knowledge of the Godhead. It takes your time to get into His word, and let it keep your heart blameless by growing in your relationship with God. Remember God can handle our sins, but what He cannot stand is our lack of loyalty and our adultery to other gods in our lives. We can only serve one master, and He is a jealous God, who wants us to pledge our hearts and lives to Him and stay blameless in our hearts till the end of all our days.

Prayer: Help me daily to have a blameless heart before you. Help me to keep my commitment to be your disciple and not waiver in my commitment. Give me a way to resist and stay blameless in your sight. In Christ name, Amen.

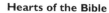
Personal Reflections: List things that are high places that you need to stay away from and overcome. Second, study 2 Peter 1:1-10 and begin to know more and more of Jesus. Write down the things in 2 Peter that you need to work on.

_____

_____

_____

_____

_____

_____

_____

_____

_____

_____

_____

_____

_____

_____

_____

_____

_____

_____

_____

_____

_____

_____

Transgressing Heart (Psalm. 36:1)

"Transgression speaks to the ungodly within his heart; there is no fear of God before his eyes."

As a believer reading this, you may say, "Is this heart for me to be concerned with since I am a believer?" Yes, it is important that each believer is aware of the world's heart to be able to understand why they act the way they do. Now we are all practicing sinners at one time, but those who grew up in a godly home or church has not had such exposure to this godless kind of thinking or acting. Therefore, it is hard to relate to those who have no fear, or conscious about doing wrong things. You may think, how can they not see right from wrong? How can they disregard others and do evil before God? You must realize they do not care who they hurt, nor do they have a heart for God. But you may be a believer who did not grow up in church and can remember or may even still struggle from time to time with the past ungodly upbringing and lifestyle before you became a disciple. You may say this was me once, but not now since I have Jesus in my heart I left this behind. If so, then thank God. It is important never to forget where you came from or be proud that you were never like them if you grew up in the church. For once you judge you become just as guilty. Is there hope for these people who were raised in an ungodly environment and have only seen this type of behavior? Yes, I think anyone who wants to come out of darkness can if they choose. The problem is; they do not want to because they are ungodly due to their unbelief. This type of person must get to a point where they are so desperate that there is only one way to go, and that is up. Unfortunately, it is hard to soften a depraved heart, so keep on praying for we are not God. Somehow, someone, or something must bring the fear to their life. Pray for those who need their hard hearts softened so that they will believe, fear the Lord, and commit to be His disciple. Remember, the first place they will see God is in you.

Prayer: Lord, use me to touch their hard heart with your love. Help me never to come to the point of hardness or lack of fear and awe of who you are, and knowingly transgress against you in my life. In the name of Jesus, amen.

Personal Reflections: Why is it important that a person fear the Lord? List any transgressions or sins you need to confess and repent of your sins. List and pray for those you know who have hard hearts. Seek out a way to show them Christ Love.

Disciplined Heart (Proverbs 23:12)

"Apply your heart to discipline, and your ears to words of knowledge."

In the book of proverbs, the goal of the writer is to bring about change through knowledge, not just delivering flowery speeches or wise sayings, but rather a application of what you have learned. Any good teacher has a goal that the student will apply what they learn. Every good preacher has the hope that the people will go away from church service and do something with what was preached. But most often that is not the case. Some people need to be disciplined like we see in verse 13. Some are bent on going against the knowledge of the truth. When they do they will suffer consequences of that rebellion. We see four aspects in this verse. First, is to apply. Go into any study with the attitude that I am going to try and learn something that I can apply to my daily life. That is why I wrote the book, "My PACT with God" This is one such book that will help you apply Scripture to your everyday life. If you do not then in most cases, you have wasted your time. Second, the heart must be motivated to learn and apply. If you do not have a heart for something, then you do not have a motivation or passion, and you will not see a need to apply what you are hearing/learning. The third aspect is discipline. Most people are not expected to carry through with the application or be committed to doing so. They may have a want or need to, but they have not been taught to be disciplined, or again not have a heart or passion. If so they will not apply the fourth aspect in this verse, and that is knowledge. What knowledge do you seek? God wants us to have the heart to study and apply the Word of God in one's life. You can have the first three, and still study the wrong set of information and you still will go down the wrong path. When you learn to discipline yourself to study and apply the Word of God you will grow in your walk. It is important first to pray for a heart of passion for discipling and applying what you learn.

Prayer: Lord, give me the heart to be disciplined, to apply your knowledge, in my life. In Jesus name, Amen.

Personal Reflections: Ask yourself, are you a disciplined person? Ask yourself, do you want to be a disciplined disciple? If yes, then pray for that passion. Who can you go to help you be disciplined? Write down some things you need disciplined in. Find someone to help be partners in Disciplined with you.

_____

_____

_____

_____

_____

_____

_____

_____

_____

_____

_____

_____

_____

_____

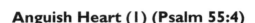

Anguish Heart (1) (Psalm 55:4)

"My heart is in anguish within me, and the terrors of death have fallen upon me."

You may say to yourself, "I do not want to read this one it sounds so bleak and discouraging." To tell you the truth, life is sometimes bleak and discouraging. If we are to be overcomers, then we must deal with the world around us in a healthy, productive way. To understand this verse, we must read verse 3 along with it. If verse 3 does not describe our world today, then we must live in a fairytale land. The voices are loud and clear against those who proclaim allegiance to Christ. No longer do we walk around in this world feeling safe. The enemy of terrorism is everywhere we go. If we claim to be a follower, then we will have a cross on us as the Jews had their star. Because of this onslaught of evil against the children of God, it is easy to see how one can be anguished in heart. In verses 5-8 the psalmist, as I, too, have thought of escaping to a safe place. Get on my 747 wings of a dove and fly somewhere safe so I do not have to deal with the impending problems. God does not always guarantee us a safe place if we are His followers. You can see this for all those then, and now, who suffer for their faith. On the other hand, God has a safe place under His wings. In verses 16 - 18 we see our hope. Calling on the Lord is our only way to survive in this world of hate. "He will hear us and redeem our soul in peace from the battle which is against us." Remember were not of this world we are just passing through. Each one of us must deal and live in this world, becoming overcomers while we are here. What can you do to help others have this same hope in God? If you have no hope, and only anguish or fear, then those around you will too want to run and hide, ignoring the battle and the victory we have in Christ. Deal with the anguish of the secular world and trust in Jesus.

Prayer: Lord, hear my voice and redeem me in this world of hate and death. I only have one hope, and that is in You. You are my strength and shield. Help me to dwell beneath your wings of love and protection.

Personal Reflections: Write down some feelings you have when you hear bad news. How do you react? Write down some things you can do to combat your feelings of fear and anguish.

_____

_____

_____

_____

_____

_____

_____

_____

_____

_____

_____

_____

_____

_____

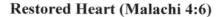

Restored Heart (Malachi 4:6)

"And he (Elijah) will restore the hearts of the fathers to their children, and the hearts of the children to their fathers, lest I come and smite the land with a curse."

This heart scripture is the last promise and prophecy of the traditional Old Testament. He (Elijah) is to restore the hearts of the fathers to the sons, and the sons to the father. This assumes there is a need for restoration between the fathers and sons. Look at your family and those around you. How are relationships between the fathers and sons in your family and your friends' families. Many statistics show that most men in jail today have little or no relationship with their fathers. If they do, usually it is one of abuse or neglect. In many cases, the father was never in the picture. Where does the problem lie in these dysfunctional families? One can assume the father has given up his responsibility and chosen not be involved, or if he were he present he may not be a real role model for his son. Some men are not allowed to be involved due to the women's choice, and tha,t too, is a problem. It is important to talk to the men who have not stepped it up over the years. If you are the father, I implore you to take charge and restore your relationship with your son or daughter. You may have to humble yourself and say, "I am sorry." If you are a child who has been damaged and offended, it may take forgiveness to approach your father. I implore you to lovingly confront your dad, or, at least, tell him how you have been hurt. It takes someone with courage, love, and the help of God to make the restoration. No matter who is at fault restoration is the goal. The Bible does warn if there is no honor there is no blessing. Malachi says there is no restoration and there will be a curse both nationally and within individual families. It takes the whole community to see this problem resolved. The mothers, fathers, children and even the church must all play a part.

Prayer: Lord, help me to restore my relationships with family and friends. If I need to be restored, help me find the courage. If I need to restore a relationship, then show me how. In Your name, amen

Personal Reflections: Are you someone who has had pain in the past with your father/mother or Son/daughter? Then make an effort to be restored, if you do you will be blessed, if not you won't. Pray for a plan to make it happen and write it below.

_____

_____

_____

_____

_____

_____

_____

_____

_____

_____

_____

_____

_____

_____

_____

Morning Star Heart (1 Peter 1:19)

"And so we have the prophetic word made more sure, to which you do well to pay attention as to a lamp shining in a dark place, until the day dawns and the morning star arises in your hearts."

In my opinion, this is one of the most amazing verses in the Bible. First, this is a prophecy. To who and when are the questions we must ask ourselves. Before we answer, a more crucial question is who or what is the morning star? When we look at other references to the morning star, then we must conclude that it is Jesus. Revelation 22:16 declares this fact. Numbers 24:17 describes Jesus as a star from Jacob. In Revelation 2:28 Jesus says that He will give "him" the morning star. "Him" refers to the angel of Thyatira. This means that Jesus will give himself to the church since He is the morning star. Therefore, when we apply this conclusion that Jesus is the morning star in the verse above, then we see that Jesus <u>may</u> arise in our hearts. The prophecy is to us who believe and follow Jesus. There should be a point in time in every believers journey that God's light shines in their dark place. What is the dark place in your life? Everyone must be aware there is a dark part in each person. When you see the darkness then the light can be seen. The dark place is the sin in one's life. You must see that you're a sinner before you can see the light. A key phrase is "pay attention." God wants everyone to pay attention to the shining light in their heart. When a person does, then on that day the morning star will arise in that person's heart. Jesus will arise in the hearts of those who pay attention to the lamp. The Star Jesus will arise in your heart if you will only let Him. Has that day dawned in your life? It is not a one-time event. The initial dawning is the day you followed Jesus, but Jesus wants to be present each day in your heart flooding you with His light and presence. The day dawns when you repent and let the light shine by following Him.

Prayer: What a great promise you give me, Lord. Guide me each day by your light and presence that lives within me. Help me to pay attention as each day dawns and you arise in my heart. Amen

Personal Reflections: Remember and describe the day you followed Jesus. How did you feel the presence of the Morning Star? Describe now how the Star,s presence helps you each day.

Petitioning heart (Psalm 119:58)

"I entreated Your favor with all my heart; be gracious to me according to Your Word."

To entreat is to go before the Lord with your petition or request. The intent of this verse is to come before the Lord first with passion. Passion is Inherent in the word entreat. It is not asking passively, but with fervor expecting to receive. Do not just go through the motions or say traditional prayers that some other person or ecclesiastical order teaches you to pray. Pray from the heart and mind. It does not have to be eloquent, but it must be sincere. A halfhearted prayer will seed and harvest little or no results. You must ask for God's favor, not expecting you should get it, but having an attitude of humbleness and not a right. He can grant your request or not. Our attitude is important in our approach to God. It is the one who is in power that grants favor, not the servant. God wants to give us favor because He loves us. But, that does not negate our responsibility to approach Him the right way. You must ask according to God's Word. God, like our earthly parents, would not lovingly grant us a request that would harm us. It is up to each one to study the Word, so you know the right request to make. God has revealed in His Word what we will receive if we will only seek Him and entreat him with passion. Do you have a list of petitions or request? Sadly, most Christians never come before the Lord with their petitions of faith. Some come to God only when they need something selfishly. Requests for spiritual needs should come first, then other people's needs, and last your personal needs. The need to be an obedient disciple, loving others, and seeking God's will is the base of God's power in your life. When you apply the spiritual disciplines in your daily life you will then be able to live a victorious life. God will be gracious to us when approach Him with a sincere and passionate heart.

Prayer: Lord, I entreat you to hear my prayers. I know you love me and want the best for me. Please teach me in your Word the petitions I should make. Thank you for your favor and grace.

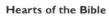

Personal Reflections: Before you approach God's throne pray for passion. Second, make petitions or list things God wants you to do to grow from your study in the Word. Then list some needs of others. Do not forget to pray prayers of thanksgiving and adoration.

_____

_____

_____

_____

_____

_____

_____

_____

_____

_____

_____

_____

_____

Peaceful Heart (Colossians 3:15)

Let the peace of Christ rule in your hearts, to which indeed you were called in one body, and be thankful"

Peace on earth is a common desire in most men's hearts. What is peace? Peace can be different for different people. Peace is the absence of strife, the absence of stress, the absence of opposition. Peace is where we want to go to rest and be assured we are safe. Can we have peace on earth? Can we have the assurance of all the stress and strife? It seems impossible in this world of selfishness and control by others that this peace can be realized. Man has striven for peace from the beginning and has not truly found it within himself or society. Many at times have seasons where they might find moments of peace, but it is fleeting or stolen away by others and conditions around us. Where can we find this peace? Or can we? Is there another aspect of peace we have not fully understood, but need in our lives? Jesus said, "Peace I leave with you" peace that passes all understanding. What is the peace of Christ? When you're in a situation of hopelessness, then the peace of knowing that Christ is in you brings you peace. Know that I can do all things through He who strengthens me, and I know that nothing can come my way that I cannot handle because I have the peace of Christ. Peace comes through the hope and faith in Jesus, and the knowledge we have the Holy Spirit in our lives to give us that peace. We cannot fully comprehend God's peace because we have yet to be fully in His presence. While we can experience some of that peace now through faith, it will not be until we are with Him in eternity that we truly understand what pure peace is all about. Peace is fleeting when we fail to rest in Him and His promises daily. In hard times, remember to call upon God to give you His peace. Without oneness in the body you cannot have peace with Christ.

Prayer: Thank you, Lord, for your gift of peace in our lives. Help me to lean on your peace even when times are not so peaceful. Take us each day to your place of peace. In your name, amen.

Personal Reflections: What things in your life seem to steal Christ's peace? What things can you get rid of, or do to have peace?

_____

_____

_____

_____

_____

_____

_____

_____

_____

_____

_____

_____

_____

_____

_____

_____

_____

_____

_____

_____

_____

_____

Willing Heart (Exodus 35:5)

Take from you a contribution to the Lord; whoever is of a willing heart, let him bring it to the Lord's contribution; gold, silver, and bronze."

The context is specifically talking about an offering of tangible things: gold silver and bronze for the purpose of building the first tabernacle. We see some interesting things that apply for today. In this chapter, the writer shares the will of the Lord for His people. God is calling His people to come with willing hearts, not hearts of compulsion or response to harsh commands. He is calling everyone to participate in this creation. The Lord is setting the principle of working six days and resting on the seventh, but this is not an option but a command. God wants His people to participate in the building process, but He wants it to be from their hearts. Even today God wants his people to serve willingly with their gifts and talents, but this is not a call that many are moved to act upon. God's kingdom needs to be built, and he desires each of us to be moved and willing to come forward with our possessions and talents and give to the task. Sadly, in most churches the pastor is expected to do all the work while the congregation sits and watches. Maybe a few will volunteer, but most are comfortable just sitting back and being served. That is not what kingdom life is in the church. Each person was called to give something and do something. What are you giving or doing in the kingdom on earth? But be assured that silver or gold is not precious to God, but the heart that seeks and serves Him willingly. Are you willingly serving with your spiritual and physical gifts? If not, then you are not following Him. What does that say about your faith and Christianity? God does not like spectators. The church is not for the individual rather for the community. Individuals should willingly give of their possessions, time, and lives of devotion so that the church may grow.

Prayer: Lord, give me a willing heart to serve you. Move me to give all I have in love for you and others. Help me to understand that all I have is yours. Thanks, Dear Lord.

Personal Reflections: List some talents and possessions you can give to God in His kingdom on earth. Are you willing to give of your time, talent, and spiritual gifts? If not, why not? If not, then are you His faithful disciple?

_____

_____

_____

_____

_____

_____

_____

_____

_____

_____

_____

_____

_____

_____

_____

_____

_____

_____

Christ's Heart (Ephesians 3:17)

" So that Christ may dwell in your hearts through faith, and that you, being rooted and grounded in love."

How does Christ dwell in our hearts? This verse gives us a start in understanding and experiencing Christ dwelling in our hearts. We usually think of dwelling in the Holy Spirit, but here Christ is also included. It is hard to understand the Godhead and how that Godhead reacts with us. Let us focus on Christ. First, we see that faith is the place to start. Faith in Christ puts us in contact with Him. Without faith it is impossible to please Him. If we do not please Him by having faith, then Christ will not dwell in our hearts. He will not come into an un-faithful heart. Is this true or false? The second thing to do is to be grounded in love. How do we get grounded in love? We must determine where love comes from? True Godly (agape) love comes from God. But how are we grounded in such love? Love is the essence of who Christ is, so to be rooted in love is to both be in love with Jesus and others. In first epistle of John we see the disciple of love; that if we love Him, we will obey Him. If we say we love Him and do not love our fellow brother or sister, then the love of Christ is not in us. Paul is trying stress that Jesus wants to make His presence known in our hearts. He wants to live with us forever, but do we want 100 % of Christ in our lives? Faith is based partly in something we do not fully see or understand, but we can understand that Christ is love; and we can trust Him and be grounded in Him. Are you grounded in love through faith in Him? How is this done? We see in verse 16 that we must be aided in this by the indwelling of the Holy Spirit which He has given each of us who become His disciple. Can we be grounded in love by ourselves? No, that is why we need the Holy Spirit. Even our coming to faith is a product of the Holy Spirit in our lives. Ground all that you do in love and the Godhead will be with you.

Prayer: Dear Lord, I come to you in childlike faith. I ask you to ground me in your love, so that I know your love and share your love with others through the power of Your Spirit. In your name.

Personal Reflections: Describe how the Holy Spirit helps you to be grounded in love. What things do you need to be grounded in through love?

Lawful Heart (Psalm 40:8)

I delight to do thy will, O my God; Thy law is within my heart."

There are jewels of impact in each phrase in this short verse. Which comes first, the delight, the law, or God? Most would say the "my God." When we acknowledge that God is my God, then we are on the path to embracing the other aspects in this verse. What does it mean to say, "my God"? The possessive proposition is in reverse. The text is not saying He is my God like we say, "my car" or "my money," but it should be a declaration that if He is my God, then I am His possession, I am His object of love. If He is "my God," then I will naturally delight in pleasing Him in all aspects of my life. Our relationship is not one of coercing or fear, but of choice. This choice and commitment should be one of delight if we truly know and understand God and who He is. Not only is He my/your creator, but the lover of my/our soul. We delight in something because it is a pleasure to do so. Do you have pleasure in loving, serving and following God? It is easy for some to serve and do things for God, but not have a delight in it. Do we do things because we feel an obligation, or because we feel the love and grace of God? We are obligated to a point, but if it is only by obligation, then we do not truly understand the relationship that God wants with us. Our delight should be in doing His will. Doing His will should be a wonderful thing and not a drudge because His will for us is for our benefit. We now come to the important part, and that is having the Law within our hearts. What law? Not all the regulations that were added by priest, rather the one that grace replaced with the Law of love for God and man. For something to truly be in one's heart, one must put the law there. How do we do such a thing? We learn by dwelling on the law both day and night. His laws are not meant to burden us but to teach us, how we should be like in Him. When a law is in the heart, it should be precious to us. We choose to put God's law in our heart so that we can honor God.

Prayer: Lord, thank you for putting your law of love in my heart. I ask you now to help me to delight more in doing your will. I pray this in your precious name, amen.

Personal Reflections: What do you delight in? Is there a time when God's will is more important than what you delight in? Should they be the same?

_____

_____

_____

_____

_____

_____

_____

_____

_____

_____

_____

_____

_____

_____

_____

_____

_____

Treasured Word in Heart (Psalm 119:11)

"Thy word I have treasured in my heart that I may not sin against thee.

In verse nine, we see that the theme is "how does a young man keep his way pure." There are a lot of gurus giving their wisdom of how one should live. But all fall short of the teachings of the Word of God. Verse eleven gives more insight for this treasure. Just knowing the content of the Word is not enough. Many learn facts and information without any change. You can be a Bible Bowl winner and a Bible college scholar, and not make any difference in ones' life. In this verse three things fulfill the way to purity for a young man. The first is to shift from the wisdom of the world to the Word of God. The Word teaches what it means to be pure in the sight of God. Trusting and depending on God's Word is the beginning to purity. The second factor is realizing it is not mere believing, but truly treasuring that Word. Treasure is a very valuable thing, and it is also subjective to the possessor or want-to-be treasure hunter. What does it mean to treasure the Word? If it is valuable to you, it is your treasure. I am afraid that most believers do not treasure the Word because they are not in it, and they do not abide by the Word. One reason is most do not treasure the word of God over their time, money, and own desires. Why do most believers not treasure the Word? The easy answer is that it is not in their heart of hearts. When one has Jesus in their heart, they will hide His word in their heart. When they do, they will become purer day by day. What is your treasure? How do you treasure it? You must spend time in the Word. I confess I too must check my treasure chest to see that God's Word is there and at the top. What fills your chest? What does your heart treasure? Is it God, Man, or yourself? God and His Word is one. Treasure them. When you do then you will have eternal rewards.

Prayer: Dear Lord, through your Spirit please help me treasure, hiding your Word in my heart. Help me not to make excuses for not treasuring your Word.

Personal Reflections: How much time do you spend in the Word or in devotions? Describe three things that you treasure in the Bible?

_____

_____

_____

_____

_____

_____

_____

_____

_____

_____

_____

_____

_____

_____

_____

_____

_____

_____

_____

Final Reflections: Ask yourself, what did you learn in this first volume of three? I hope you began to see what lies in the heart of God. You can only begin to understand when you know His heart. For you to do this you need to begin to see what lies in the heart of man, both good and bad, and what happens when you learn what God wants in your heart. It is important to have a heart that is willing to be transformed by God's heart. I hope you will continue knowing God's heart by studying more in my other volumes.

What is in your heart? Do you know? Do others know? Be for sure God knows.

What is in God's heart? Do you know? God knows if you do or don't.

God wants you to know both your and His heart, and He wants you to live by what you know. This is what you will learn when you read and use this book of Biblical hearts.

Coming Soon

Hearts from the Bible Volumes Two and Three,

Please contact:

Michael Householder at mikerhouseholder@gmail.com to find out when the next volume is ready to ship.

And please take some time to explore Dr. Householder's other books at

www.fishnetpublishers.net

"Children with His heart"

and "White as Snow" were written and performed by Michael R. Householder on his album "Spirit Warriors" recorded in Moscow, Russia while he was a missionary there. His whole album is available from Fishnet Publishers PO Box 20606 Knoxville, TN 37940 or on our website at

www.fishnetpublishers.net

Michael's second album "New Wineskins" was recorded in Poland while he was serving as a missionary. "New Wineskins" is an album of Michael's favorite hymns, and may be your favorites too. Songs include; His eye is on the sparrow, He is Lord, What a friend we have in Jesus, Heavenly Father, Oh how I love Jesus, and especially his rejoice medley will have you praising the Lord.

Take a look at Dr. Householder's other books!

The Most Precious Thing in the World

10 Steps to Spiritual Growth

The Church Growth System

Walk in Discipleship Volumes 1 & 2

My Pact with God Journal

Please see www.fishnetpublishers.net

and our ministry site at
www.globalchurchgrowth.blogspot.com

Index to all three volumes_____

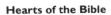

221

Made in the USA
Middletown, DE
13 August 2024

58653835R00126